BILL SEVERN'S
IMPROMPTU MAGIC

BILL SEVERN'S
IMPROMPTU MAGIC

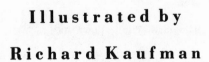

Illustrated by

Richard Kaufman

CHARLES SCRIBNER'S SONS

New York

Library of Congress Cataloging in Publication Data

Severn, Bill.
  Bill Severn's Impromptu magic.

  Includes index.
  1. Conjuring. 2. Tricks. I. Title. II. Title:
Impromptu magic.
GV1547.S486 1982   793.8   82-7331
ISBN 0-684-17606-8   AACR2

1 3 5 7 9 11 13 15 17 19   F / C   20 18 16 14 12 10 8 6 4 2

Printed in the United States of America.

CONTENTS

4. MIXING PLEASURE WITH BUSINESS

5. WITH BORROWED MONEY

6. SECRET DEVICES

INTRODUCTION

The word *impromptu* is defined in Webster's as "done on, or as if on, the spur of the moment." Impromptu magic takes full advantage of the "as if" clause. It is magic that *seems* to be done on the spur of the moment, but not without some practice and preparation for it.

All good impromptu magic, the kind that is fun to do and fun for others to watch, is well planned, no matter how extemporaneous it may appear to be. Before you can perform it, you obviously must learn how to do the tricks.

Magic books that simply give the bare-bones secrets of tricks, without really teaching how to do them and how to present them, are of little practical value to those who hope to perform them effectively. It is the intention of this book to provide carefully planned and explicit instructions, with fully rounded presentations that clearly explain not only *what* to do, but *how* to do it.

Here you will find dozens of tricks the average person easily can learn to do with simple props put together wherever he or she happens to be. This is magic with the most ordinary objects, with everyday things and those borrowed from viewers or carried in pockets or purse. The tricks require no elaborate "magic show" equipment and no lengthy advance preparation, although some preparation usually is necessary.

All the tricks are based on performance-tested methods long used by magicians, adapted to enable the amateur to present them wherever a few friends are gathered—in a home living room or kitchen, at a party, at the card table, after lunch or dinner, with business companions, during an office coffee break, or outdoors at a picnic or around a campfire.

But far more important than the tricks is the presentation of magic—surrounding the trick with a story plot, acting it out, building up a magical surprise that converts it from a mere puzzle into entertainment. Good presentation is what is most often lacking in the routine performance of impromptu magic.

It is hoped that this book may help by furnishing some novel, interesting, and amusing magical plots; suggested "patter"; and pointers on timing, handling, what to emphasize to put the effect across, and how to direct the attention of those watching so they see only what you want them to see.

With each trick, there are suggestions for *Other ways to do it*, variations in the presentation, method, or props, additional routines, and ideas for creating new tricks from those already learned.

There is also a chapter explaining prearranged small props and simple devices you can have with you when you perform, which can be secretly used to turn apparently impromptu tricks into mystifying feats that would be difficult to accomplish without them. This chapter of secret devices includes complete routines for a wide range of tricks in which these devices are used.

Throughout the book, each trick begins with *How it looks*, so that while you are learning the trick, you can keep in mind the presentation and the effect it should have. This is followed by *The set-up*, explaining the props that are needed, and how they are prepared and arranged. Then the detailed step-by-step handling, performance, and presentation are given in *What you do*. Finally the trick, props, method, and other presentations or uses for them are explored in *Other ways to do it*.

This is an informal book. Although related tricks are grouped by chapter, there has been no attempt to confine all tricks of a particular kind to a single chapter.

The reader especially interested in tricks with coins and bills, for instance, will find instructions not only in the chapter on money magic, but also in the chapters on card tricks, on tricks with office things, and on tricks with secret devices. If your special interest is in card tricks, you will find some of the best of those in the chapter on secret devices. As another example, there is no separate chapter on mental magic, but such tricks can be found in all the chapters. This is because each trick that is explained includes basic moves, methods, or secrets that can be used with other props of various kinds. Altogether there are more than one hundred tricks, routines, and variations.

This is also an informal book because impromptu magic is informal. There is no "magician" and no "audience" in the theatrical sense of a "performer" putting on a full magic act for "spectators." These are tricks that are meant to be done one or two at a time by you for your friends under mainly close-up conditions and, most of all, just for fun.

I hope you will have fun with this magic, and the pleasure of making it fun for others to see.

CHAPTER 1

MAGIC AT HOME

Imagine That!

HOW IT LOOKS

You ask a few friends who are visiting your home to take part in a little game for the fun of testing their imagination. "We'll need an empty chair," you say, and you pick up a small chair and place it in the middle of the room.

"Now I want you all to imagine that there is someone seated in this chair," you explain. "It could be a man, a woman, a child—just try to picture someone in your mind. Concentrate on the chair, and visualize that person turning a little in the chair, shifting position, looking around to stare back at you."

You are standing a few feet away from the chair, not moving, and with your hands at your sides. But as you speak, the empty chair moves!

It slowly inches around on the floor by itself. You quickly place it in another position, then step back from it, and stand still again.

"Can you *see* someone there?" you ask. "Someone pushing back the chair—getting to his feet?" The chair pushes back by itself, and then turns itself around again.

You lift the chair away, return it to the spot you first took it from, and say, "If you think you saw what I think you saw—then you *do* have a vivid imagination."

THE SET-UP

The fun of this trick depends more on how you present it than on the method. It is done in a very simple way: with a loop of thread. Ordinary fine black thread can be used, but the chair should not be placed directly beneath a bright overhead light; subdued side wall lighting is best. The floor should be smooth-carpeted, or uncarpeted, so the chair will slide easily.

You will need a small, lightweight straight-backed chair, either one that usually stands against the wall as part of the room furniture or one that you can quickly bring into the room from a bedroom or kitchen.

Take a two-yard length of black thread and tie the two ends together, knotting them several times, to form a loop. Put one end of the loop up over the chair's left front leg. Hang the other end, with the loop spread open, down over the back of the chair. Stand the chair against the wall, where it will be out of the way until you are ready to use it.

WHAT YOU DO

Introduce the trick as "a little game to test your imagination." Say, "We'll need an empty chair," and walk across the room to get it. (If you plan to bring it in from another room, just add, "I'll go get one we can use.")

As you face the chair and bend down to pick it up, bring your left hand to the left side of it, near the seat. Put your thumb under that side of the thread, hooking the thread in the crotch of the thumb. Close your thumb to grip the thread, and then take the left side of the chair with your left fingers. Take the right side of the chair with your right fingers, and carry it, with both hands, to the middle of the room.

Put the chair down so that it faces those who are watching, and remove your hands, keeping the thread hooked on your left thumb. Drop your hands to your sides, and step back staying on the right side of the chair, until you feel the thread drawn taut. "Now I want you all

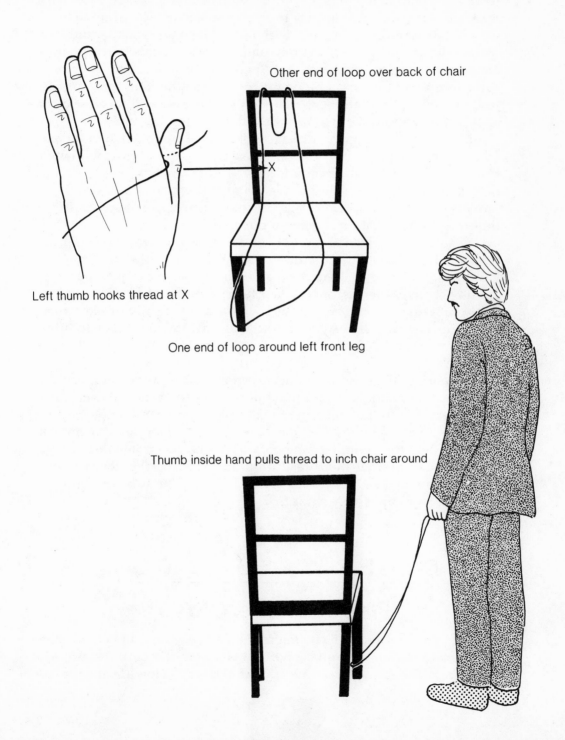

Other end of loop over back of chair

X

Left thumb hooks thread at X

One end of loop around left front leg

Thumb inside hand pulls thread to inch chair around

to imagine that someone is seated in this chair," you say. "It could be a man, a woman, a child—just try to picture someone in your mind. . . . "

Remain standing as you are, without moving your arms or your feet, with both hands kept at your sides, and ask your friends to concentrate on the chair and to visualize that "person" turning a little. Secretly, move *only your left thumb*, drawing it back inside the hand at your side. Just the slightest pull on the thread with your thumb will inch the chair around enough to surprise those who are watching it intently.

Now, still keeping the thread hooked over your left thumb, and with that hand at your side, turn and take the top of the chair with your right hand. *Slide* the chair around on the floor to change its position, until the front of it is toward the left, and its back is toward you. (This turns the thread around the legs, so that when you secretly pull the thread again, the chair will seem to turn itself around.)

"Can you *see* someone there?" you ask, as you move away until the thread is taut. "Someone pushing back the chair—getting up from it?" Work your thumb to pull the chair, and quickly move back another step, as if to get out of the way as the chair turns. Don't overdo it by attempting to drag the chair back and forth. Just make it turn once, and then pick it up and carry it away, standing it against the wall. "If you think you saw what I think you saw," you say, "then you *do* have a vivid imagination."

As you put the chair down against the wall, place your right hand on top of the chair's back and pull your left hand away from the chair to *break* the thread, but keep the broken thread still gripped with your left hand for a moment. With your hands at your sides, and the broken thread trailing from your left fingers, walk half a dozen steps away from the chair, and *then* let the thread drop unnoticed to the floor. If your friends want to look the chair over—and they probably will—they won't discover any telltale thread.

OTHER WAYS TO DO IT

Ghost in the Closet

"I don't believe in ghosts," you tell friends who are seated in your living room with you. "But the other night I was up late, sitting here reading, and I heard the strangest sounds in that closet over there." You get up and walk over to a closet, grasp the knob, and open the closet door. "When I looked inside—I didn't see anything there."

You close the door again, and stand back from it. "But it was what happened then that made me wonder if we had a ghost," you say. "*Something* inside the closet began to push the door open. . . ." Slowly the door begins to open by itself, turning until it stands open wide. You stare at the door for a moment, then slam it shut, and walk away from the closet. "Maybe it's only a mouse. . . . But if it is, it must be the strongest mouse in the world!"

This trick is done the same way as the preceding one, with a loop of thread. How you rig the thread depends on the kind of knob the closet door has. If it is an ordinary round doorknob, just put one end of the loop over the knob, so the rest of the thread hangs down from it. But if it has a bracket-type handle, put one end of the thread through the handle before you tie the ends into a loop. In either case, the loop should be slightly shorter than the distance from the handle to the floor.

Start by talking about your "strange experience" of hearing sounds in the closet, and then get up and walk over to the door. Facing the closet, reach for the knob with your right hand. Hook your right thumb through the right side of the looped thread, the part that hangs just beneath the knob. Then take the knob with your fingers, and step back as you open the door.

Keep your hand on the knob as you hold the door open, and say, "When I looked inside—I didn't see anything there." Close the door again, but don't shut it quite all the way; leave it open just a crack, so the latch doesn't snap. With your right thumb still hooked through the thread, take that hand from the knob and lower it to your side. Step back from the door until you feel the thread pull taut.

"But it was what happened then that made me wonder if we had a ghost," you say. "*Something* inside the closet began to push the door open. . . ." With your right hand at the side away from those who are watching, work your thumb to pull the thread so the door slowly begins to open. Step back from it, as if to get out of the way, and give the thread another secret pull to swing the door open wide.

Stare up at the door for a moment, and then place your *left* palm against it and slam the door shut, *breaking* the thread that is still gripped as it was, with your right hand down at your side. Quickly walk away from the closet, secretly drop the broken thread, and say, "Maybe it's only a mouse. . . . But if it is, it must be the strongest mouse in the world!"

Superspoon

HOW IT LOOKS

You are with a few friends in the kitchen, and you pick up a spoon and a dish towel. Holding the spoon upright with one hand, you drape the center of the towel over it, and then fold the towel around so the spoon is wrapped inside. You take the towel by its bunched ends, with the center hanging down, and as you gently shake it back and forth, the spoon visibly passes right through it and falls out onto the floor!

THE SET-UP

This quick little kitchen mystery requires no preparation. All you need are a dish towel and a teaspoon.

WHAT YOU DO

Hold the spoon by its bowl between your left thumb and fingers, with its handle standing upright. Take one end of the towel with your right hand, and shake it open. Drape the towel over the upright spoon, drawing the end that is in your right hand back over your left arm to the elbow.

Take away your right hand and bring it up to the covered top of the spoon handle. As if to outline the shape of the spoon in the towel, slide your right thumb and fingers down it, thumb at the back, until the thumb is just *below* the bottom of the spoon. With your left thumb, from inside the towel, secretly pinch a small part of the cloth in an upward fold against the bottom edge of the spoon's bowl. Keep the spoon and that fold gripped with your left thumb, and take your right hand away.

Tip your left hand over directly forward and down, until the handle of the spoon is toward the floor, and at the same time shake the towel off that hand so it hangs down from your thumb and fingers. (At the back, hidden from front view by the hanging folds, the spoon is now outside the towel. But it looks as though you are holding it inside the center of the towel.)

With your right hand, fold one side of the towel around the back of the spoon, and then the other side over that, and on around to the front. Wrap it tightly, and make sure the spoon is entirely inside the folds. Then put your right hand around the towel to hold the ends bunched together, and turn that hand over, so the towel hangs down from it like a bag.

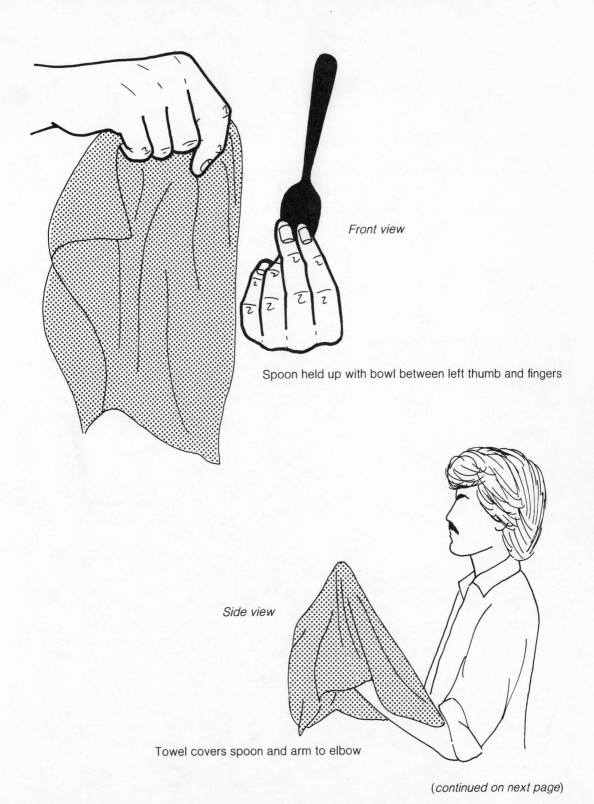

Front view

Spoon held up with bowl between left thumb and fingers

Side view

Towel covers spoon and arm to elbow

(*continued on next page*)

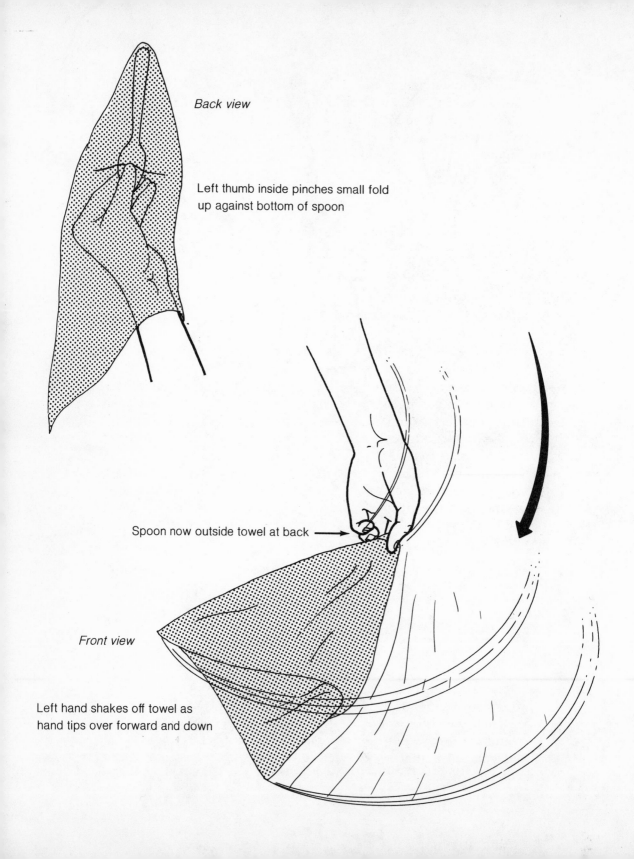

Back view

Left thumb inside pinches small fold
up against bottom of spoon

Spoon now outside towel at back →

Front view

Left hand shakes off towel as
hand tips over forward and down

Swing the towel gently back and forth, jiggling it slightly, until the spoon slides out and falls to the floor. Take one corner with your left hand, pull the towel from your right hand, and shake it open. Hold it out between both hands to show that it was undamaged by the penetrating spoon.

OTHER WAYS TO DO IT

Supercracker

You can do this trick with a saltine and a table napkin, instead of the spoon and dish towel, and seem to make the saltine pass through the center of the napkin.

Start with the saltine held squarely, not diagonally, between your left thumb and fingers at its straight bottom edge. Hold the napkin by one corner to cover the saltine, and draw a good part of the napkin back over your left arm. At the point where you secretly pinch a little fold of cloth with your left thumb, make sure the bottom of that pinched fold is below the bottom edge of the saltine. Follow the rest of the moves as with the towel and spoon.

In place of the saltine, you can use a small pretzel, cookie, or sugar packet to penetrate the napkin. Or use a pocket handkerchief, borrow a lipstick, and pass the lipstick through the handkerchief—but hold it over a table, or over the owner's hand, so the lipstick won't be damaged falling to the floor.

Comedy Thumb Escape

HOW IT LOOKS

You ask someone to bind your two thumbs tightly together with a piece of wire. Then you borrow the person's wristwatch, hold that in your fingers, and ask him or her to cover your hands with a small towel.

"Did you know that your watch is running fast?" you ask. "As a matter of fact, it has completely run away. It has disappeared." You shake the towel off your hands to show that they are empty and that the watch has vanished, even though your thumbs are still bound together.

"I'll bet you know where it went," you say. "And you're right. . . . It went up my sleeve." You push your sleeve up far enough to show that the vanished watch is on your arm. "But now we have a problem." You lift your bound thumbs. "Never mind how it got *on* my arm. . . . How am I going to get it *off*, with my thumbs wired together?"

You ask the person to cover your hands again with the towel. "I may have to keep your watch on my arm forever. I hope it's waterproofed— I mean, in case I want to take a shower. . . . Wait a minute. . . . I think I've got it!"

You suddenly bring your right hand out free from under the towel, with the watch in your fingers. Placing the watch on the table, you quickly put your hand back under the towel, and immediately shake the towel off your hands. Both thumbs are tightly bound together, as if your hands had never been apart!

"Will you please cut the wire to *free* my thumbs?" You give the owner of the watch a small pair of wire snippers that have been lying on the table, and hold out your hands so he or she can cut the wire to release your thumbs. Then you pick up the watch, give it back to the owner, and say, "Your watch is *amazed*. . . . It's holding its hands to its face."

THE SET-UP

You can use almost any thin, flexible, *covered* wire, a single strand about ten inches long. You will also need a small pair of wire snippers, or strong scissors, and a hand towel or dish towel that will cover the lower part of your arms when the center of it is draped over your hands.

There is nothing to prepare in advance. When you are ready to do the trick, just put the wire snippers or scissors, the wire, and the towel on a table that is positioned so you can stand beside it.

WHAT YOU DO

"First of all—will you all please look at your watches?" you say. You gesture by pulling up your left sleeve, as if to look at your own watch. "Everybody, please—just check to make sure you've still got them." Then you look out at the group and smile. "Thanks a lot. If I were a pickpocket, I'd know now just where to look for a good one."

Aside from the joke, this gives you a chance to glance around quickly and see who is wearing a watch with an expanding link band, because that is the kind you will need to borrow, *not* one with a leather buckle strap. Choose a person you now know is wearing such a watch, and ask him or her to stand next to you. Pick up the wire, show it, and say, "I want you to bind my thumbs with this wire."

Bend the wire in half, and put the center around the base of your right thumb. Cross the ends against the left side of that thumb by bringing the top end down *across the front* of the bottom one. Now put the side of your left thumb up against the side of your right thumb, to hold the crossed wire between them. Keep your thumbs together, and use your right fingers to push the lower end of the wire up through the crotch of the left thumb. (This takes only a second, and you do it all quite openly, as if you were just putting the wire around your thumbs so they will be tightly bound. But crossing the ends this way provides enough slack so that you can instantly get your right thumb free, no matter how tightly the wire is tied.)

"Please pull the ends out tight," you say, keeping the sides of your thumbs pressed together as you turn to the owner of the watch. "Tie them together to fasten them just as tightly as you can."

When he or she has finished tying the wire, lift your hands to show your bound thumbs all around. Now ask to borrow the watch. Put your right fingers through the band, closing them to hold the watch band on your hand. Then ask the owner to take the towel from the table, shake it open, and drape the center of it over your hands. Jiggle the towel around on your hands if necessary, to make sure it also covers the bottom end of the right sleeve of your jacket.

The way your thumbs were fastened has left the wire around them in the shape of a horizontal figure eight, with the two thumbs in the loops, and the wire crossed between them. All you have to do to get your right thumb free is to dip it down toward the front, and turn it a little to the left. This opens the loop enough to give plenty of slack, so you can quickly draw your thumb out.

With your hands under the towel, free your right thumb, and with your left fingers pull the watch up your right arm beneath the sleeve of your jacket. Now, to bring your thumbs back to their original bound position, simply put your right thumb back down through the loop you took it from, and lift that thumb up beside your left thumb again. This draws the loop tight, as it was at the beginning.

Step close to the table, hold your covered hands over it, and shake the towel off them so it drops to the table. Open your palms to show that your hands are empty and that the watch has vanished, even though your thumbs are still tightly bound.

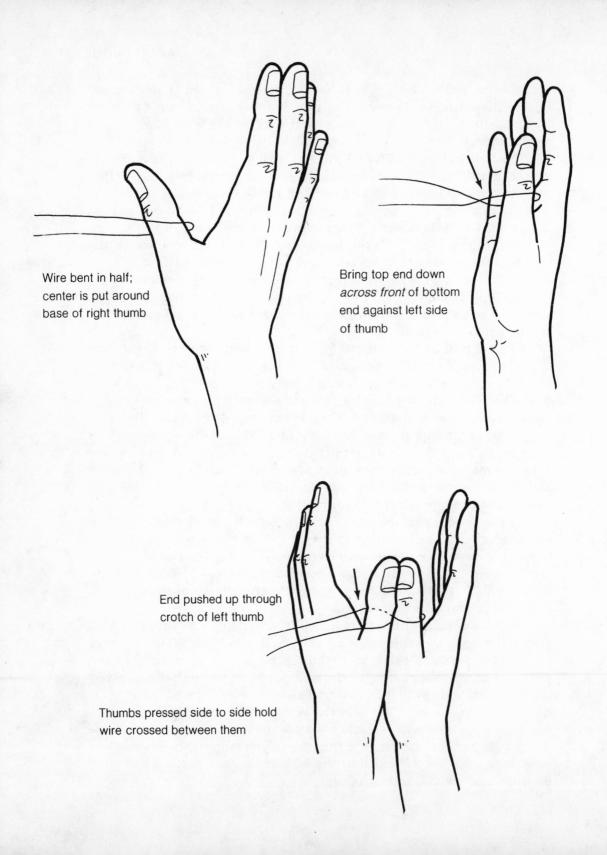

Wire bent in half;
center is put around
base of right thumb

Bring top end down
across front of bottom
end against left side
of thumb

End pushed up through
crotch of left thumb

Thumbs pressed side to side hold
wire crossed between them

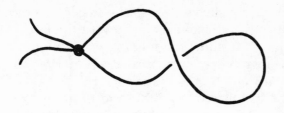

Wire in a figure eight shape around thumbs
after ends are pulled tight and tied

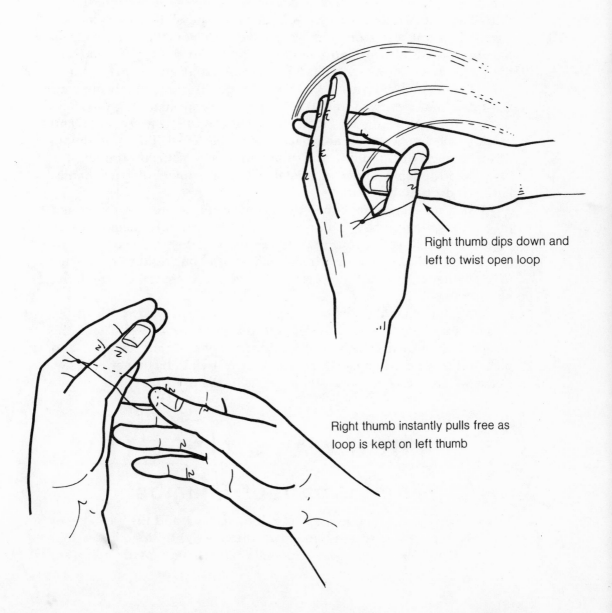

Right thumb dips down and
left to twist open loop

Right thumb instantly pulls free as
loop is kept on left thumb

Pause a moment, and then say, "I'll bet you know where it went. And you're right.... It went up my sleeve." Press the inside of your right sleeve against your body and slide your hands toward the left, so the sleeve is pulled up far enough to show the missing watch on your arm. "But now we have a problem. Never mind how it got *on* my arm. How am I going to get it *off*, with my thumbs wired together?"

Ask the person to take the towel from the table and to put it over your hands again. Make sure it covers the lower part of your sleeve. With your hands under it, as you joke about the possibility that you may have to keep the watch on your arm forever, free your right thumb from the wire loop. With your left hand, reach into your right sleeve and pull the watch down into your right hand, closing your fingers to hold it.

"Wait a minute," you say. "I think I've got it!" Suddenly bring your right hand out free from under the towel. Lift your hand high to show the watch in your fingers. Place the watch carefully on the table, and quickly put your empty hand back under the towel. Put your thumb down through the loop, lift that thumb up beside your left thumb, step back from the table, and immediately shake the towel off your hands, letting it drop to the floor.

Lift your hands to show that your thumbs are tightly bound together, as though they had never been apart, and hold them that way for a moment. Keeping your thumbs pressed together, move both hands to the table and pick up the wire snippers with your right fingers. Turn to the owner of the watch, and say, "Will you please cut the wire to *free* my thumbs?"

Hold out your thumbs so the person can cut the wire. When the thumbs are free, rub them a little, as if to restore circulation. Thank the owner of the watch, take back the snippers, put them on the table, and pick up the watch. Glance at it as you give it back to its owner, and say, "Your watch is *amazed*.... It's holding its hands to its face."

OTHER WAYS TO DO IT

The Turnabout Thumbs

You take a raincoat from a closet, toss it on a chair, and then ask one of your visiting friends to bind your two thumbs tightly together with a piece of wire. When he or she has done that, you say, "Will you please pick up the coat and put it around me? Just hang it loosely over my shoulders."

You turn your back so your friend can do that. But as he or she lifts the coat toward your shoulders, you suddenly step away. "Never mind," you say. "It's already happened!"

What has happened, as your viewers can see, is that instead of being bound in front of you, your two hands are now behind your back, with your thumbs still wired together.

"As you can see, my thumbs are still tightly bound," you tell them, "which means that my hands must have passed right through my body. . . . But if they did—I didn't feel a thing." You ask the person helping you to look in the pocket of the coat. "You'll find a pair of wire snippers. Will you take them out, please, and cut the wire to *free* me?"

This instant escape and rebinding of your thumbs with the wire is done by the same method used in the preceding trick. To set it up, just put a small pair of wire snippers (or strong scissors) into one of the raincoat pockets, and hang the coat in a closet. Have the piece of wire in one of your own pockets.

When you are ready to do the trick, take the coat from the closet, toss it on a chair, and take the wire from your pocket to show it. "I want you to bind my two thumbs tightly together with this piece of wire," you say. Bend the wire, cross it around your thumbs as previously explained, and ask your friend to pull the ends and tie them as tightly as possible.

Then ask your friend to pick up the coat and to hang it loosely around your shoulders. Turn your back, and immediately release your right thumb from the wire. Wait until he or she has opened the coat and started to lift it toward your shoulders, and then quickly slide both hands around your sides, keeping them against your body as you bring them together behind you.

Point the tops of your thumbs *in toward your back*, put your right thumb down into the loop, and lift it against your left thumb to tighten the wire around both thumbs. As you do that, suddenly step away from your friend, and say, "Never mind. . . . It's already happened!"

The lifting of the coat toward your shoulders helps to distract attention and to screen your hands as you are quickly sliding them around behind you, making for a more dramatic surprise. But it doesn't really matter if some of those watching see you shift your hands from front to back. They will still be puzzled and amused by the quick escape and the instant rebinding of your thumbs.

Take a few steps to one side, so everybody has a clear view of your hands behind you. Joke about having passed your hands through your body. Then ask the person to remove the snippers from the coat pocket so he or she can cut the wire to free you.

The Flying Plastic Bag

HOW IT LOOKS

You show three clear plastic food storage bags, put one aside, and tie the other two together by their corners. Tucking them into your pocket, you leave the ends hanging out in full view. Then you roll up the third bag, snap a rubber band around it, and hold that in your closed hand.

"Two here," you say, tapping your pocket. "And one here." You hold up your closed hand. "Now watch this one fly!" Suddenly you make a throwing motion toward your pocket with your hand, and that bag vanishes, leaving your hand empty. "Gone!"

You pull the other bags out of your pocket, whipping them up into the air, and the vanished third bag appears tied between those two. "And there it is—tied between!"

THE SET-UP

You will need a small rubber band and four clear plastic food storage bags, gallon size (11½" × 13").

To prepare them, turn all four bags with their bottom edges to the top. Pick up each bag in turn and hold it by one corner, so the rest hangs down as if you were holding a handkerchief by one corner. Run your other hand down along each bag several times, to take out some of the stiffness and to shape it diagonally.

Tie two of the bags together, corner to corner, with a *small* square knot. Place them on a table, and fold one over on top of the other so they lie together. Turn the bags diagonally, with the knot at the top, and bend that knot down toward you.

Starting just below the knot, fold the upper bag vertically back and forth upon itself in one-inch accordion pleats, loosely gathering in the sides of the bag as you fold it. When you have pleated it to within about three inches from its bottom corner, fold that bottom corner straight up to the top, over the pleats, so the corner extends well above the knot. Wrap the side edges of the lower bag around the pleated bundle by folding the right edge over and across it, and then the left edge over and across that.

Hold the bags pressed together, and lay the diagonal top corner of another bag directly on the top corner of the first set. Then lay the corner of the remaining bag, in the same way, on top of those. Fasten the rubber band around them, down over the top corners and around the pleated part, to hold the bags diagonally stacked together.

You can keep them fixed that way in a drawer or on a cupboard shelf until you want to take them out and show the trick.

WHAT YOU DO

Hold your left hand up with its palm toward you, and place the stacked-together bags in that hand. The secretly tied set should be at the bottom of the stack, against your fingers. Close your fingers loosely around the bags, with your thumb across to hold them. Three top corners stick up above your hand.

Remove the rubber band from around the bags, and put it on the table. With your right hand, take the first bag from the stack. Shake the bag out so the audience can see it, then put it aside on the table. Take the second bag with your right hand, and hold that one up with your fingers around it, palm toward you, and with its top corner sticking up above your hand.

(At this point, you appear to be holding a single bag in each hand, but your left hand really is holding the double set. The pleated part is hidden inside that hand; the top corner of the hidden bag, sticking up from the hand, makes it look from the front as if it were all one bag.)

Bring your hands in front of you, and tie the corners of the two bags together with a square knot. Show the knot to your audience, and then bend the knot back toward you into your left hand, to hold that part of the bags bunched together. Grip the bags in that same place with your right hand, and take them with that hand. Tuck the bunched part of the bags down into your breast pocket, leaving the other two ends hanging out of the pocket in full view. (If you aren't wearing a jacket with a breast pocket, tuck the bags into the waistband at the front of your pants or skirt.)

Now pick up the remaining bag from the table. With both hands, wad it into a tight little ball. Take the rubber band from the table, and fasten it around the wadded bag. Hold the bag up to show it, by turning

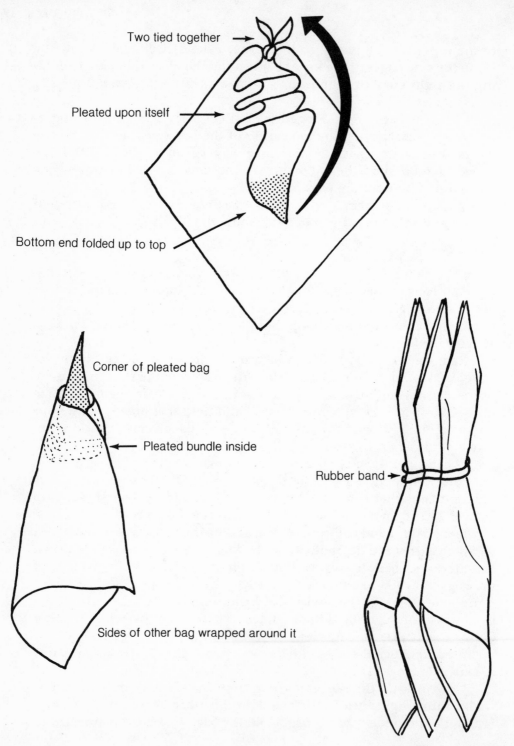

Two tied together

Pleated upon itself

Bottom end folded up to top

Corner of pleated bag

Pleated bundle inside

Sides of other bag wrapped around it

Rubber band

Bags stacked together

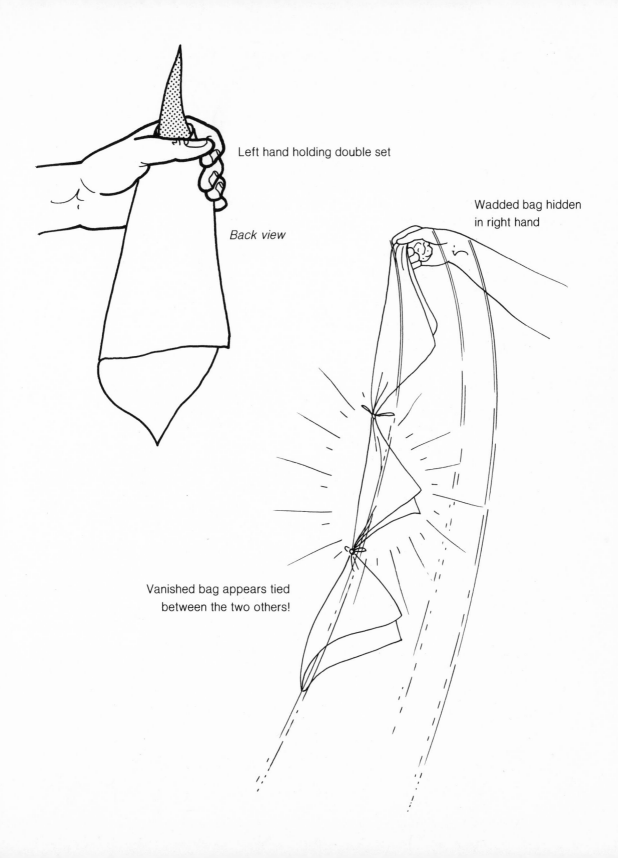

Left hand holding double set

Back view

Wadded bag hidden
in right hand

Vanished bag appears tied
between the two others!

your right-hand palm upward with the wadded bag held between your thumb at the back and your fingertips at the front. The right palm should be cupped beneath it, with the back of the hand toward the floor.

Turn your left hand palm down, and bring it down over the top of your right hand, as if to take the wadded bag between your left thumb and fingers. But with your left hand momentarily covering the right one, let the bag secretly drop from your right fingertips into the cupped right palm. Close your left fingers as if *they* had the bag, and lift the closed left hand away, turning your head to look at that hand.

Immediately bring your right hand over to your breast pocket, with the back of that hand toward those watching, and with the wadded bag hidden in it. With your right thumb and first finger, grip one corner of the bags hanging down from the pocket. Lift the corner up a little, and keep it held out between your right thumb and finger.

Tap your left fist against your breast pocket, and say, "Two here." Hold your closed left hand out to the left again, and say, "One here." Make a sudden throwing motion toward the pocket, and open the left hand wide to show it is empty. "Gone!"

With your right hand, pull the bags up out of your pocket by the corner still gripped between your thumb and finger. Whip them up into the air, and give them a hard downward shake so the pleated one instantly opens out and appears knotted between the other two. "And there it is," you say, as you hold up the chain of three. "Tied between!"

Finally bunch all the bags up into the right hand, and put them away with the wadded one that had been in that hand.

OTHER WAYS TO DO IT

Bagged Again

Here's a somewhat easier version of the trick. It eliminates the need to vanish the wadded bag from your hand. You make it disappear from your pants or skirt pocket instead, and at the end you are left with nothing concealed in your hands. Also, instead of tucking the two tied-together bags into your breast pocket, you put those into a plastic tumbler.

You will need an opaque plastic tumbler or a tall coffee mug. Have one or the other on your table at the start. The bags are prepared the same way as previously, and diagonally stacked together with a rubber band around them.

Hold the stacked bags in your left hand as before. Remove the rubber band, and put that on the table. Take the first bag from the stack, shake it open to show it, and put it aside. Take the next bag from the stack, hold it in your right hand, and tie the top corner of it to the top corner of what seems to be the single bag still in your left hand.

Bunch together the knotted part, and take the bags with your right hand. Put the bunched part down into the bottom of the tumbler on the table, leaving the other ends hanging out. Pick up the remaining bag from the table, wad it into a tight ball, and snap the rubber band around it.

Show that bag with your right hand, and then openly put it into your right pants' or skirt pocket, as you say, "And this one goes into my pocket." Bring your hand out to show it is empty. With your left hand, pick up the tumbler. Hold the tumbler up to the left of your body.

Put your right hand back into your pocket, quickly close your lower fingers around the wadded bag to hide it in them, and grip the bottom of the pocket lining between your thumb and first finger. Pull the pocket inside out, and, *without letting go of the part gripped between your thumb and finger,* hold it pulled out. Shake the lining gently to show the pocket empty, then push it back in and remove your hand, leaving the wadded bag in the pocket. (This pocket dodge is explained in detail in Chapter 3, *The Two Fastest Tricks in the World.*)

"Gone!" you say. "Did you see it fly?" Bring your empty right hand up to the tumbler your left hand is holding. Take one corner of the bags, pull them out of the tumbler, and whip them up into the air. "There it is—tied between!"

Sealed Thoughts

HOW IT LOOKS

You ask your friends to join in a "psychic experiment" to see how close you can come to guessing a particular thought someone has in mind. "We all have dozens of different thoughts running through our minds all the time," you explain, "so let's pin this down to one simple and specific group of words that we can decide on entirely by chance."

You place a book, a pair of dice, an envelope, and a pen on a table, and then ask one person to hold the book while another shakes the dice and rolls them out. "Do that several times," you say. "Keep rolling out the dice until you feel like stopping."

The number your friend finally rolls may be an eight. "All right," you say. "Eight is our chance number." You turn to the person who has the book. "Will you look through the book until you come to the beginning of chapter eight? Then read the first few words of that chapter to yourself. Clear your mind of everything else, and concentrate on those first few words."

You pick up the pen and envelope, take a blank card from the envelope, and slowly print something on the card. Then you slide the card back into the envelope, seal it, and drop it on the table. "Now that we have a sealed record of my impression of your thoughts," you say to the person with the book, "for the first time, will you please read those words aloud?"

Your friend reads out the chosen words from the book. You pick up the envelope, tear it open, and ask someone to draw out the card and read aloud what you wrote on it. Your written impression matches the words in the book!

THE SET-UP

Although there seems to be a possible choice of many words, it really is limited to the words at the beginning of chapters two through twelve, because those are the only numbers that can be rolled with a pair of dice. Those words are secretly written in advance on the inside flap of the envelope. This takes only a few minutes to prepare.

You will need a book with clearly numbered chapters, preferably a currently popular novel with a well-known title. Take an envelope, open the flap, and with a pencil print the number 2 inside the flap at the top left, just within the gummed part used to seal it. After that number, print the first few words from the beginning of chapter two of the book.

Continue to do the same thing with each of the other chapters, on through twelve, printing the words in numbered horizontal rows across the flap and on the inside part of the envelope that the flap will cover. Make the printing large enough to read easily, but don't run it out on the gummed edges.

Slide a blank 3" × 5" index card or a slip of stiff paper into the envelope. Crease the flap shut without sealing it. Turn the envelope face up, and put it with the book, dice, and pen, so you can place them all on a table when you are ready to do the trick.

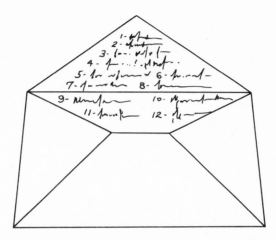

Words written on flap and on part flap will cover when shut

WHAT YOU DO

Introduce the "psychic experiment," and explain that you want to "pin it down to one simple and specific group of words that we can decide on entirely by chance." Give one person the book, and ask someone else to shake the dice and to keep rolling them out on the table until he or she is satisfied with whatever number finally comes up.

Call out that "chance number," and ask the person with the book to look through it "until you come to the beginning of chapter eight" (or whatever the number happens to be), and then to read silently the first few words of that chapter.

While your friend is doing that, pick up the envelope, hold it with its back toward you, and open the flap. Glance at and remember the words for that numbered chapter. Remove the blank card, close the flap, and lay the card on the envelope. Hold card and envelope with your left hand, and pick up the pen with your right hand.

Close your eyes a moment, pause as if you are concentrating on your friend's thoughts, and then hesitantly print the remembered words on the card. Lift the envelope with its back toward you, open it, slide the card into it, and lick the flap to seal it shut. Press your thumbs across to make sure it is tightly sealed.

Toss the envelope on the table, and say to the person with the book, "Now that we have a sealed record of my impression of your thoughts—for the first time, will you please read aloud the words in the book?"

Pick up the envelope, hold it high, and walk to some other person in the group. Tear a strip off the *end* of the envelope, squeeze the sides to open it wide, and tilt it down so that person can reach into it and remove the card. Casually crumple the envelope and put it into your pocket to discard it. Ask your friend to read aloud your "sealed thoughts," the words you wrote on the card, to confirm that they match the words chosen by chance from the book.

OTHER WAYS TO DO IT

Scribble Scrabble

Instead of the card and envelope, you can do the trick with a small pad of paper. Turn back the first sheet without tearing it off the pad. Print the book chapter numbers and first words of each chapter in a vertical row on the second sheet, and then put the blank first sheet down over it. Have the pad lying on the table with the book, dice, and pen.

Start the same way, by giving someone the book, having another person roll the dice, and then asking the one with the book to turn to the chapter of that number and to look at the first few words. Now pick up the pad, hold it in your left hand with the face of the pad toward you, and say, "I'll try to get an impression of the words you have in mind."

Write *any* word or two on the pad, then shake your head, tear off the page, crumple it, and discard it by putting it into your pocket. That leaves the second sheet with the secretly printed words from the book facing you on top of the pad, which you keep lifted toward you. Glance at it to get the information you need, and again start to write something on the pad, *writing right across the words already there.* Halt, shut your eyes, and say, "No . . . I still haven't got it."

Rip that second sheet from the pad, crumpling it as you do so, and discard it by putting it into your pocket. "Please concentrate on just the first word," you tell the person with the book. "Then think of the second word, and the next one. . . . Think of one word at a time."

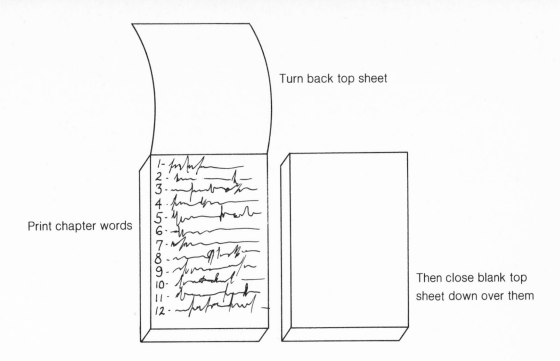

Turn back top sheet

Print chapter words

Then close blank top sheet down over them

You are now left with a clean pad. Slowly print the right words on it. Tear off the sheet, fold it once, and drop the pad on the table. Go to someone in the group, give the person the folded slip, and ask him or her to hold it for a moment. Have the first person read aloud from the book, and then ask the other person to read aloud the words you wrote on the slip of paper.

Book Choice

You can start the trick by offering a seemingly free choice of any one of three different books, instead of only a single book. That is done by means of an old but effective dodge known as *magician's choice*, which really gives the person no choice at all.

Have the book you want your friend to choose on the table with two others, and say, "Will you please remove two of those books?" If neither of the books he or she picks up is the one you want chosen, just take them and put them aside as you say, "All right, we'll eliminate those two." Then hand your friend the one remaining on the table, which is the book you want to use.

But if one of the two books picked up is the one you want chosen, you say, "Now hand me either of those two." If you are handed the right one, hold it up, and say, "All right, we'll use this one then." But if you are handed the wrong one, put it on top of the other one on the table, push them aside, and say, "Very well, we'll use the one you kept."

Then go on with the trick as you would if you had started with only a single book.

CHAPTER 2

PARTY TIME

Chips Coming Up!

HOW IT LOOKS

This is the instant production of a small bag of potato chips from a sheet of newspaper. You pick up the paper, unfold it, show both sides are empty, and fold it again. When you tip it over, the bag of chips appears by sliding out of the paper into your other hand.

THE SET-UP

You need a double sheet (two attached pages) of a tabloid-size newspaper, or a newspaper magazine section, and a small single-serving "snack pack" bag of chips. These are about 4½" × 6", light in weight, and fairly flat. If there are no "snack packs" available, put some chips into an ordinary plastic sandwich bag, fasten it with a twist tie, and use that.

So that the attached newspaper pages can be folded easily in either direction, close the paper and crease the centerfold hard with your thumbnail, then fold the top page around to the back, and crease the centerfold again.

Open out the paper on a table. Turn the bag of chips with its long sides top and bottom. Lay it on the opened left-hand page, about three inches down from the top and an inch in from the left edge. Close the right-hand page over it from right to left, and then turn the left edges to the bottom, toward you at the back of the table. That is the position it should be in at the start of the trick.

Have the newspaper where you can quickly pick it up. There should be nobody watching from directly behind you.

WHAT YOU DO

Turn your left-hand palm *up*, and bring that hand to the paper at the open edge that is toward you. Slide the left fingers underneath the paper and the thumb inside, so the thumb goes in over the end of the hidden bag of chips to hold it.

Turn your right-hand palm *down*, and take the edge of the top page between the right thumb inside and fingers outside. Keeping the hands together, lift the paper up in front of you, turning it vertically upright, and then spread your hands apart to open it out.

Show it that way for a moment, held open between your hands, with your left thumb holding the bag of chips hidden behind the edge of the left page. Now fold the right page *out away from you*, around to the front and all the way over to the left. Place the edge of it between your left first and second fingers to hold the paper with your left hand.

Take what is now the back page with your right hand, gripped between your fingers down inside the top edge and your thumb at the back. With your right hand, quickly pull that back page horizontally *straight out toward the right*, opening it out all the way from left to right. This pulls the back page from under the bag of chips, which is left where it was, held by the left thumb behind the paper's left edge. You have now shown both sides of the paper are empty.

Close the right page again by folding it toward you from right to left. Press your right fingers against the back of the paper to keep the bag of chips in place for an instant, and move your left thumb out to hold the paper with the bag pinched between the pages.

Bring your right hand to the bottom of the page and loosely fold the paper up in half from bottom to top. Take the paper at the top with

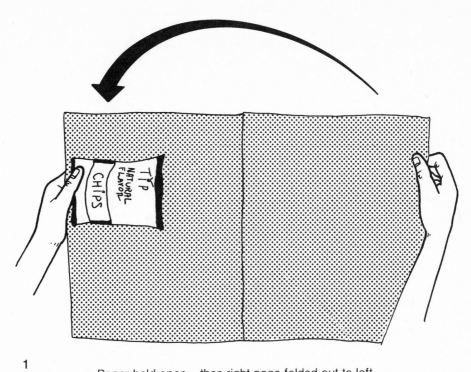

1 Paper held open—then right page folded out to left

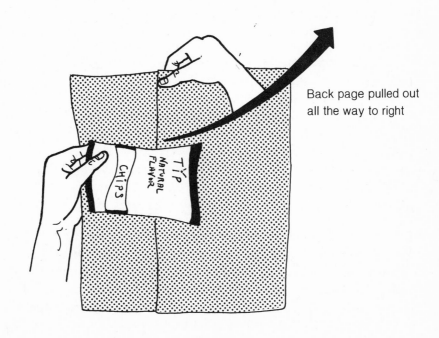

Back page pulled out
all the way to right

2

your right hand, and remove your left hand. Tip the open edges downward, and slide the bag of chips out of the paper into your left hand.

OTHER WAYS TO DO IT

There's My Hat!

Hide a small folded paper party hat in the newspaper instead of the bag of chips. Handle the paper in the same way as previously. Hold it opened out between your hands, and ask, "Did you ever try to make a hat by folding a sheet of newspaper?" Fold the right-hand page out around to the front, then look at it and shake your head. "No, that's wrong. . . . I think you fold it the other way."

Pull the back page out to the right, and pretend to be confused as you fold the paper again, after having incidentally shown both sides empty. "Oh, the heck with it. . . . It's a lot easier to do with magic." Snap your fingers, reach into the folded newspaper, and produce the party hat. Quickly unfold it, put it on your head, and say, "There's my hat!"

Did Somebody Lose a Sock?

Fold an old sock in half, and tuck the toe end down inside the top so it will stay held together. Flatten it as much as possible, and hide it in the newspaper the same way the bag of chips was hidden.

Show the paper is empty, and then produce the sock from it. Pull the sock open, hold it dangling from your fingers, stare at it, and say, "How did that get there? It was supposed to be a handkerchief." Pull up the legs of your pants, look down at them, and say, "I was afraid it was one of mine, but it isn't. . . . Did somebody lose a sock?"

Lunchtime

Make a thin sandwich, put it into a plastic sandwich bag, and fasten it with a twist tie. Hide it in a newspaper with the bottom of the bag toward the opening, so it will be easy to grip between your left thumb and fingers when you pick up the paper. Handle the paper as before, to show quickly it is empty. Then fold the paper, tip out the sandwich, and say, "I brought my own lunch."

Cigam

HOW IT LOOKS

You take two paper party napkins from your pocket, roll one of them into a ball, and ask someone to hold it. Then you tear the other napkin to pieces, roll up the pieces, and say the word "Magic!" When you open it out, the torn-up napkin is whole again.

"It's much harder, of course, to do the trick backward," you say, "but I'll try." You ask the person to whom you gave the first rolled-up napkin at the start of the trick to hold that out on his or her hand. "I'll just say the word 'Cigam.' That's 'Magic' spelled backward—and if it works, instead of the whole napkin you started with, yours should now be ripped to pieces. . . . Will you open it out, please, and let's see?"

The person unrolls the ordinary whole napkin that he or she has been holding all the while, and discovers that it *is* torn to pieces!

THE SET-UP

You need three small paper party napkins. Tear one into four pieces, and wad the pieces into a tight ball with no torn edges showing. Put the other two still-folded napkins into the left-hand pocket of your jacket, and drop the wadded ball of torn pieces into the same pocket with them.

WHAT YOU DO

Reach into your pocket with your left hand. Close your lower three fingers around the ball of torn pieces to hide it in them, leaving your thumb and first finger free. Bring out the two folded napkins. Take the top one with your right hand, and put that on the table, or tuck it partly into your jacket pocket to leave it there momentarily.

Open out the other folded napkin. Take one top corner between the thumb and first finger of each hand, and hold it spread out between them, with the backs of the hands toward those watching. With the help of your right hand, crumple it into a ball, wadding it into your left hand.

As you do that, with your right fingers inside your left hand, switch the crumpled whole napkin for the ball of torn pieces. Just leave the whole napkin in your left fingers, hidden from front view by the back of the hand, and take the other napkin instead between your right thumb and first finger. Hold that napkin up to show it, and let your left

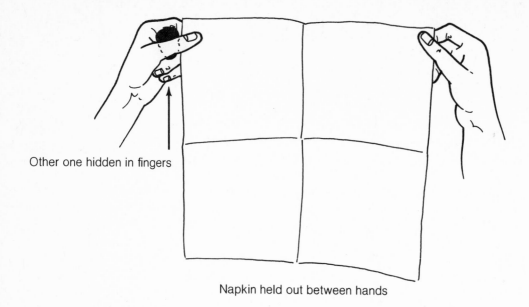

Other one hidden in fingers

Napkin held out between hands

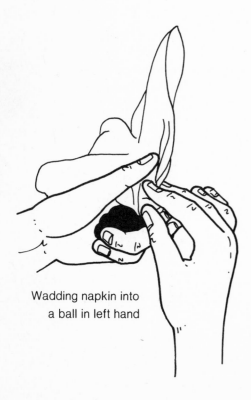

Wadding napkin into
a ball in left hand

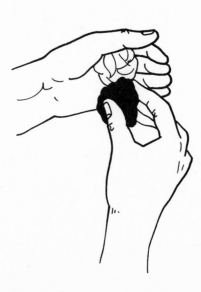

Inside left hand—right hand switches them

hand fall to your side with the whole one now hidden in your loosely closed left fingers.

Ask someone to hold out a hand. Put the ball of torn pieces into it, and say, "Will you please keep this one for a minute? Just close your fingers around it, and don't let it get away."

Pick up the second folded napkin with your left thumb and first finger, and use both hands to open it out. As before, take one top corner between the thumb and first finger of each hand, and hold it spread out between them. Bring your hands together, with their backs still toward those watching, and quickly tear the napkin in half, then in half again.

Crush the torn pieces into your left hand as you wad them into a ball. With your right fingers inside your left hand, switch the ball of torn pieces for the crumpled whole napkin that was hidden in the left hand, leaving the torn one hidden there instead. Hold up the rolled whole napkin between your right thumb and first finger, and let your left hand fall to your side.

Look at the napkin in your right hand, and say, "Magic!" Bring your hands together, open out the napkin to show it is whole again, and keep it opened out for a second. Then loosely crumple it into your left hand, and discard it by putting it into your pocket, leaving the torn pieces in the pocket as you bring your empty hand out again.

"It's much harder, of course, to do the trick backward," you say, "but I'll try." Turn to the person. "Do you still have the napkin I gave you when we started all of this? Will you hold out your hand and open your fingers, please? I'll just say the word 'Cigam'—that's 'Magic' spelled backward. . . . *Cigam!*" Wave your right hand over the person's hand, but don't touch it. "If it works, instead of the whole napkin you started with, yours should now be ripped to pieces. Will you open it out, please, and let us see?"

Let the person unroll the napkin and discover that it is torn to pieces. Take the pieces, hold them up, and say, "First the torn one whole again, and now the whole one torn. . . . That's magic in reverse!"

OTHER WAYS TO DO IT

Sympathetic Torn Napkins

You show a party napkin, tear it to pieces, roll the pieces into a ball, and ask someone to hold that. Then you take a second napkin, tear that one to pieces, and crumple those pieces into a ball. You wave your hand over the torn pieces, open them out, and show that the napkin is whole again.

"What happens to one," you say, "also happens to the other." You ask the person who has been holding the first ball of torn pieces to open it out. When he or she does, that napkin also is whole again.

For this trick, you will need four small paper party napkins. Crumple two of them into tight balls, and put those into your left jacket pocket with the two separately folded napkins.

Start the trick by putting your left hand into your pocket. Get one of the crumpled balls hidden in your fingers, leaving the thumb and first finger free, and bring out one of the folded napkins. Open it out to show it held between your hands, and then tear it in half, and in half once again.

Crumple the torn pieces into a ball, switching the ball of pieces for the whole one as previously explained. Take the whole napkin between your right first finger and thumb to hold it up and show it. Let your left hand fall to your side with the torn napkin hidden in it. Ask someone please to hold out a hand. Put the whole napkin, the one everybody thinks is torn pieces, into the person's hand, and tell him or her to close that hand.

Now reach into your pocket again with your left hand. Drop the torn pieces, get the second crumpled whole napkin hidden in your fingers, and bring out the other folded napkin. Open it, hold it out between your thumbs and first fingers, and then tear that in half, and in half again. As you crumple the pieces into a ball, switch them for the whole napkin. Move the whole napkin up to hold it between the tips of your left thumb and first finger to display it, keeping the torn one hidden inside your other left fingers.

Lift your empty right hand, wave it over the napkin as if casting a "magic spell," and then open out the napkin to show that it is whole again. Hold it spread out between your hands for a second. Loosely crumple it up into your left hand and put it away in your pocket, leaving the ball of torn pieces in the pocket with it.

"What happens to one," you say, "also happens to the other." Ask the person to open his hand and unroll the "torn pieces." Let your friend discover that that napkin also has been restored. Take it, hold it up to show it, and say, "Magic can happen anywhere. . . . In your hands as well as mine."

Toot Sweet

HOW IT LOOKS

You roll a paper napkin into a ball, place it on the table, and cover it with a cone-shaped cardboard party horn. Very slowly and deliberately, you lift the horn, stand it to one side, and pick up the paper ball. You put the ball away in your pocket, then lean down over the horn that is standing upright on the table and blow down into it, sounding a loud toot. When you lift away the horn, the paper ball has reappeared under it.

Once more, you show the horn is empty, stand it to one side, pick up the paper ball, and put that away in your pocket. You blow through the horn that is resting upright on the table; then, when you lift away the horn, instead of the rolled-up napkin, a dollar bill appears!

THE SET-UP

Blowing through the horn not only provides a sound effect to herald each of the magical changes, but also automatically accomplishes the first part of the trick. Any of the usual small cardboard cone-shaped party horns can be used. (If it is *very* small, use napkins torn in half instead of full-sized ones.)

Find some opportunity ahead of time secretly to roll one of the napkins into a tight ball. Drop the ball into the horn, and push it down until it is wedged inside close to the mouthpiece. You may want to use a pencil to wedge it in tightly.

Crumple a dollar bill into a ball, and put that into the right-hand pocket of your jacket. Make sure there is a duplicate paper napkin handy. Have the horn standing upright on the table, or lying there with its mouth toward the back.

WHAT YOU DO

This routine is best done silently, except for the toots on the horn. Roll the duplicate napkin into a ball, place it on the table, and let it be seen that your hands are empty. Stand the upright horn over the paper ball to cover it.

Doing it all slowly and deliberately, lift the horn again, give it a little downward shake to indicate that it is empty, and stand it upright

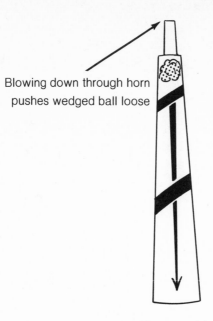

Blowing down through horn
pushes wedged ball loose

Horn on table

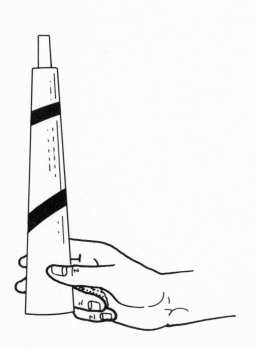

Hand steadies horn on table

Bill rolls out of fingers

to one side. With your right hand, pick up the paper ball, show it, put it into your jacket pocket, and bring your hand out. Put the thumb and first finger of that hand around the horn near the bottom to hold it steady on the table.

Lean down over the horn, keeping it on the table, and blow through the mouthpiece to sound the horn. Blow hard. The push of air will dislodge the wedged napkin so it falls to the table inside the horn. Lift the horn high to show that the napkin you put into your pocket apparently has reappeared under the horn.

Again, shake the horn to show it is empty, and stand it upright on the table. Pick up the rolled napkin, show it, and put it into your jacket pocket. With your hand inside the pocket, drop the napkin and scoop the crumpled bill into your hand, hiding it by closing your lower fingers loosely around it, leaving the thumb and first finger free. Bring your hand out, and put your thumb and first finger around the bottom of the horn, as if to steady it on the table as before.

Lean down over the horn, keeping it on the table, and blow down through the mouthpiece to sound it. Open your lower right fingers to let the hidden bill roll out of them onto the table as you lift the horn high. The bill seems to have rolled out from under the horn, suddenly appearing there. Put down the horn, and open out the bill to show it.

OTHER WAYS TO DO IT

Blow Out

In this version, a small paper ball vanishes from your pants or skirt pocket and seems to fly through the air to reappear under a party horn standing on the table. "I'll do it again," you say. "This time, very slowly." You repeat the trick, and once more the ball disappears from your pocket. But when you lift the horn, it *isn't* there.

"Too slow," you say. "It's still flying invisibly through the air." You show your hand is empty, and pretend to catch the ball and toss it invisibly into the horn that the other hand is holding. You lift the horn to your lips and toot it loudly. The missing paper ball flies out of the horn, up into the air!

You will need the same kind of small cardboard party horn and three half-napkins, each crumpled into a tight ball. Secretly wedge one of the paper balls down inside the horn, so it is held in place close to the mouthpiece. Turn the horn mouth upward, and drop a second paper ball into it, loosely, on top of the first one. Keep the horn, mouth upward, in one of the inside pockets of your jacket or in your purse, until you are ready to show the trick. Have the third paper ball in your otherwise empty right-hand pants or skirt pocket.

Start the trick by saying, "I thought of this one while I was waiting in line for a bus." Take out the horn and lay it on its *side* on the table, with its mouth away from those watching. Reach into your pants or skirt pocket, bring out the paper ball, and put that on the table. "Did you ever wish you could just fly through the air to wherever you wanted to go?"

Pick up the horn with your right thumb and fingers close to its mouth. Squeeze the cardboard slightly, so the loose ball doesn't fall out, and stand the horn upright on the table on its mouth. Pick up the paper ball, show it, and put that into your right pants or skirt pocket. Bring your hand out, show it is empty, and say, "I haven't worked it out yet for humans—this is just a scale model, of course."

Snap your fingers in front of your pants or skirt pocket. Then reach into the pocket and close your fingers around the paper ball to hold it in them, leaving the thumb and first finger free. With the thumb and first finger, grip the bottom of the pocket lining and pull it inside out, *without letting go of it*. Keep it held out that way for a moment, pinched between thumb and finger, and shake the cloth a little to show the pocket is empty. Then push the lining back in, leaving the hidden ball in the pocket as you take your hand out empty.

"It has flown from there...." Move your hand above the horn on the table and snap your fingers. Lift the horn, and show the first of the duplicate paper balls, which has fallen down to appear under it. "And here it is." Offer to do the trick again. "This time, very slowly."

Shake the inverted horn to indicate that it is empty, and stand it upright on its mouth again. Slowly pick up the paper ball, put it into your right pants or skirt pocket, and bring your hand out. Snap your fingers in front of the pocket, reach into it, and crush both paper balls into your fingers. Grip the bottom of the pocket lining between the thumb and first finger, as before, and pull the lining inside out, holding it out to show the pocket is empty. Push the lining back in, leave the two paper balls in the pocket, and remove your empty hand.

Snap your right fingers above the horn. With that hand, lift the horn high, as if you expected the vanished paper ball to reappear beneath it. Then look down at the table and "discover" that the ball *isn't* there. Shake your head and say, "Too slow. . . . It's still flying invisibly through the air."

Take the horn with your left hand, and hold it mouth *upward*. Reach out with your right hand as if plucking the invisible ball from the air. Pretend to toss it up with the right hand and to catch it with the horn in the left hand. Transfer the horn to your right hand and lift it to your lips, tilting its mouth upward. Sound it loudly, blowing hard to dislodge the wedged second duplicate ball, which will fly up out of the horn into the air.

Band a Can

HOW IT LOOKS

You pick up a can of cola or some other drink, wrap a rubber band twice around the middle of it, and hold the palms of your hands over the ends of the can.

"When you give the command, this rubber band will pass right through the metal can and fly free," you tell someone. "Whenever you wish, just call out, 'Go!'"

The instant the person commands the band to go, it penetrates the can and pops up high into the air!

THE SET-UP

All you need is any drink can and a rubber band that fits easily around it. A large flat band is best.

WHAT YOU DO

With your left hand, hold the can horizontally in front of you, thumb on top and fingers underneath. Take the band with your right hand, and put it once around the middle of the can. Then grip the part of the band that is toward you between your right thumb and fingers, putting the four fingers in through the band from right to left. Holding it that way, stretch the band down as far as you can.

Beneath the can, secretly put the tip of the left second finger *between* the two strands of the band. Draw the top strand around the back of that fingertip, so that strand is held against the fingernail. Keep the band

Back view

1 Upper strand goes around behind
  tip of left second finger

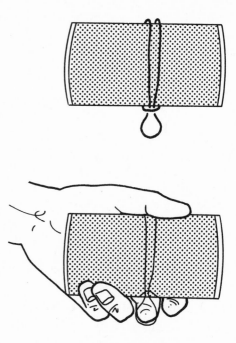

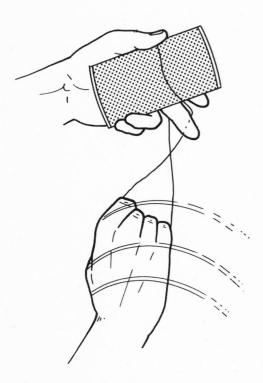

Fingertip caught inside loop as band goes
around can—pulls free to release band

Hidden under can

2 Right hand twists upper strand
  across lower—then puts its loop
  up over end of can

stretched out, and twist the right hand palm downward, which twists the top strand over the bottom strand. Now bring the part of the band in the right hand out to the right and over that end of the can, to leave it snapped around the middle of the can.

This should all be done quickly, without pausing, so it looks as if you simply wound the band twice around the middle of the can. But it really brings the two ends of the band together beneath the can, with one end drawn through the other and held tightly looped around the tip of your left second finger.

Keep your left fingers underneath the can, and hold it horizontally between both hands. Explain to someone that at his or her command, the band will "pass right through the metal can and fly free." When the person commands the rubber band to go, draw your left second finger out of the loop and release the band. It will pop off the can, and fly up into the air.

OTHER WAYS TO DO IT

The Banana Test

Instead of a drink can, you use a banana for this version of the trick. Hold the banana horizontally in front of you with your left hand. Wind the rubber band twice around the middle of the banana in the way that was previously explained, forming a secret loop around the tip of your left second finger, hidden behind it.

"I've found a way to test a banana to make sure it's ripe," you say. "If you can pull a rubber band right through it, then it's ripe enough to eat. But the trick is to do it so fast you don't cut the skin or harm the fruit."

As you speak, take *one strand* of the band between your right thumb and first finger. Quickly pull the band out and forward as you release the loop from your left fingertip, so the band comes away in your right hand, seeming to pass right through the middle of the banana, and say, "Just like that!"

More Penetrations

Either the pop-off or pull-through penetration can be used with many other commonly available objects. You might do the trick with a single-serving size box of breakfast cereal, a candy bar, a cucumber, a capped bottle of ketchup (or other bottle that can't be seen through), a can of baked beans that you say you suspect may contain "jumping beans."

You could put the rubber band around a small gift box, and explain you have invented a magical method of opening packages in a hurry by making the band fly right through the box the instant anyone wants to look inside it. In an office, you might cause the band to penetrate a stiff-backed pad of paper, a stack of business cards, a short mailing tube, or a ruler.

Keeping Away from Coffee

HOW IT LOOKS

You are seated with friends somewhere that coffee is being served. Picking up a paper napkin, you take it by two corners, hold it up to show both sides of it are empty, and drape the center of it over one hand.

"My doctor told me to keep away from coffee," you say, as you grasp the napkin with your hand. You turn the napkin over, and suddenly a full-length drinking straw appears, standing up out of the center of the napkin. As you put the straw into the cup and prepare to take a sip of coffee through it, you jokingly explain, "I drink it through a straw to keep as far away from coffee as I can."

THE SET-UP

The trick is possible because a plastic drinking straw, after being folded up small, will spring open again and can be quickly smoothed to its original shape. You will need a plastic straw and a small safety pin (about an inch long). The trick should be done where there is a paper napkin handy.

Set it up in advance by folding the straw back and forth upon itself in loose one-inch accordion folds. Keep the safety pin closed, and slide the folded straw through the middle part of the pin, so the pin holds it compressed. Have the pin, with the straw in it, in your right-hand pocket.

Folded plastic straw   Held compressed in pin

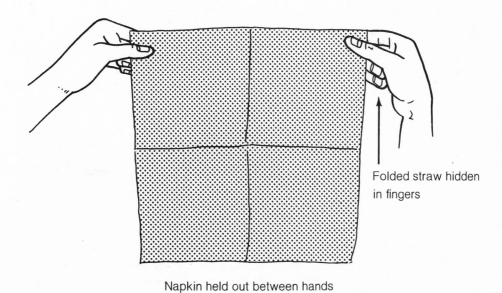

Folded straw hidden
in fingers

Napkin held out between hands

(*continued on next page*)

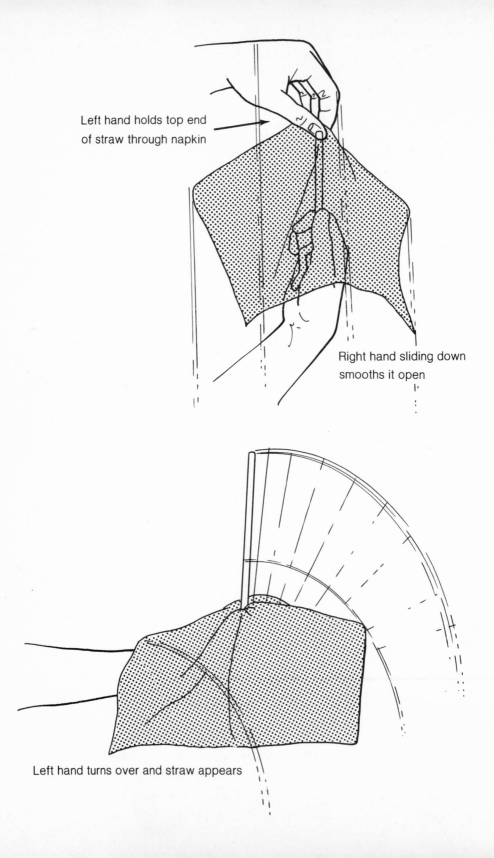

Left hand holds top end
of straw through napkin

Right hand sliding down
smooths it open

Left hand turns over and straw appears

WHAT YOU DO

Have the napkin unfolded on the table or on your lap, and shortly before you intend to do the trick, put your right hand into your pocket. Grip the folded straw, slide the pin down off it, and close your three lower fingers around the straw to hide it in them, leaving your thumb and first finger free. Bring your hand out of your pocket and let it fall to your side for a moment as you continue the conversation until the time seems right to show the trick.

Pick up one corner of the napkin between your right thumb and first finger, keeping the back of the hand toward those watching. Shake out the napkin, and take the opposite corner between your left thumb and first finger, holding that hand the same way as the right, with the napkin stretched out between them. Turn the napkin to show both sides.

Drop the corner from your right hand, and bring that hand up under the center as your left hand drapes the napkin over it. Then bring your left hand to the *outside center*, and grip one end of the straw to hold it through the napkin.

Under the napkin, slide your right hand down along the expanding straw, smoothing open the folds and rounding the shape between your thumb and fingers as they rapidly slide down it. Continue to slide the right hand on down, and remove that hand from the napkin. Quickly turn your left hand over, palm up, so the napkin falls down around it and reveals the upright straw that suddenly appears.

Do not actually drink through the straw. The coffee is much hotter when taken like this, because you don't inhale air along with the liquid as you do when sipping it the usual way, and you could burn your mouth. Just finish the trick by *preparing* to take a drink though the straw, as you explain how you keep away from coffee.

OTHER WAYS TO DO IT

Straw Vote

Instead of telling the story about coffee, you can say that someone stopped you on the street and asked you questions for an opinion poll. Then you show the napkin or your pocket handkerchief empty the same way as before, and when you suddenly produce the straw standing up at the center of it, you say, "He was taking a straw vote . . . so I gave him mine."

Fortune's Cap

HOW IT LOOKS

"Have you seen these new fortune-telling pens?" you ask, as you take a pen from your pocket or bag and show it to a few friends who are seated with you. "It's just like any other pen, except for the cap." You remove the cap, and give it to one of them to hold for a moment. "Close your hand around it and think of some question about the future that you would like to ask."

While the person holds the cap, you take the pen itself and a small square of paper. At the top left corner of the paper, you print the word YES; then print NO at the opposite corner, and MAYBE at the bottom. You take back the cap, lay it on the center of the paper, and hold the paper flat on your lap.

"Would you like to know if you are about to take an unexpected journey, if you will inherit money, if tomorrow will be your lucky day?" you ask the person. "Just for fun, let's see what this cap of fortune has to say. What is your question?"

Your friend asks the question aloud. Very slowly, the cap of the pen begins to move by itself across the flat paper, as if drawn by some mysterious force. It crawls in one direction, and then another, and finally comes to rest on one of the words that indicates a YES, NO, or MAYBE answer.

You invite one or two of the others to ask questions and to have their fortunes told in the same way. After each question is answered, you roll the cap off the paper, and handle both cap and paper freely. There is nothing attached to the paper or to your hands, and nothing "tricky" about the cap for anyone to discover.

THE SET-UP

You will need a small magnet, the kind commonly found in many homes and offices where they are used as bulletin board memo holders or to clip or hang various things. It doesn't matter if it has a decorative backing of some sort, as long as the magnet side is flat. Have the magnet

Magnet in pocket pulled up on top of leg

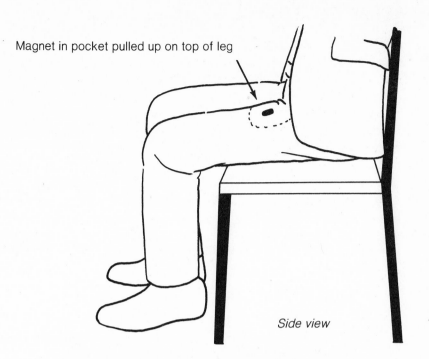

Side view

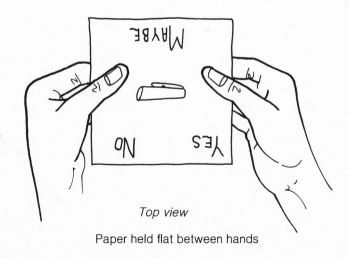

Top view

Paper held flat between hands

in the empty left-hand pocket of your pants (a pants pocket is necessary for this version of the trick), with the magnet surface toward the outside.

The pen should have a removable cap with the usual steel pocket clip attached. Clip the pen into a pocket or carry it with you in a bag. Any available blank paper can be used. You will need a piece about five inches square. Make sure there is paper handy, or else carry it with you already torn to size.

You should be seated with your friends beside you, or closely opposite you, with both your knees directly in front of you so those watching will have a clear view of the paper you hold on your lap.

Shortly before you do the trick, slip both hands into your pants pockets and secretly pull the left pocket over to adjust it so the magnet at the bottom of that pocket rests on top of your left leg. Then remove both hands.

WHAT YOU DO

Talk about the "fortune-telling pen" as you take it out and show it. Remove the cap, and ask someone to hold it in his or her hand while thinking of some question to ask about the future. Print the word YES about an inch down from the top left corner of the paper, NO at the opposite corner, and MAYBE centered near the bottom.

Put the pen itself aside, and hold the paper flat, with your left thumb and fingers at the left edge of it. Rest the center of the paper on your left leg so it is directly over the magnet hidden in your pocket. With your right hand, take the cap back from the person who has been holding it. Lay the cap on the center of the paper, with its metal clip toward the bottom, so the clip comes into contact through the paper with the magnet. (With your left fingers under the edge of the paper, you will be able to feel the magnet to make sure the cap is over it.)

Hold the right edge of the paper between your right thumb and fingers, in the same way that your left thumb and fingers are holding the other edge. Have the person ask the question.

While everyone is concentrating attention on the cap, *very slowly* extend your arms forward, backward, or slightly to either side, moving the paper gripped between your hands so the cap seems to creep across it. The slight movement of your arms creates the illusion that the cap is moving, and you can guide the motion until it finally comes to rest on the word that best "answers" the particular question.

After each question, lift the paper between your hands to break contact with the magnet, and then tilt the paper with your right hand so the cap freely rolls off it into the left hand. Casually show both sides of the paper, rest it on your left leg again, and place the cap at the center as before. But don't overdo it; two or three questions are enough.

OTHER WAYS TO DO IT

Knee Power

Instead of having the magnet in your pocket, you can have it taped to your leg beneath your clothes. It makes the trick somewhat easier to do, since you don't have to adjust in secret the position of the magnet in your pocket, and makes the effect more convincing because you can hold the paper farther down on your leg, where the presence of a magnet is less likely to be suspected. It also allows you greater freedom of movement, and leaves your pocket empty for carrying other things. But it does require a little more advance preparation.

You will need a three-inch length of cloth adhesive tape (or you can use a large Band-Aid), and a small magnet that is flat on both sides. A bar-type or button magnet is best. Fasten the magnet lengthwise to the center of the tape, making sure it is firmly fixed in place, and loosely roll up the two ends of the tape. You can carry it around that way in one of your pockets, ready to use whenever you want it.

At some time before you do the trick, step into a bathroom or another place where nobody will see you. Open out the tape, and under your clothes, fasten the magnet to your left leg just above the knee. It takes only a moment to fix the magnet in place, and you can wear it hidden that way and walk around freely before and after the trick, until you later find an opportunity to remove it secretly. Follow the same routine as before, but hold the paper over your knee instead of up over your pocket.

With a Paper Clip

For a different presentation of the same trick that seems entirely impromptu, you can borrow all the props you use (except for the hidden magnet). Borrow a pencil, a piece of paper, and an ordinary paper clip.

Put the clip on the center of the paper, on which you have printed the words with the pencil, and use the clip instead of the cap of your pen to indicate the answers by making it crawl mysteriously around on the paper.

If there are no paper clips available, any small steel object will serve: a nail, screw, little metal nut, or safety pin.

Please Pass the Mustard

HOW IT LOOKS

At a picnic or other outdoor meal, you gather some of the things that happen to be on the table, and lay them out in a row. These might include a can of cola, a jar of mustard, a cup, knife, fork, and spoon, a paper napkin. Announcing that you are about to make a prediction, you write something on a piece of paper and put it aside without showing what you have written.

"Will you join me in a little game of chance?" you ask someone. "You and I are going to take turns eliminating these things, one at a time, until only one is left. Here's how we'll do it, so neither of us can guess what that final object will be."

You put your two hands down on two of the things on the table, ask your friend to touch either one of your hands, and push aside whatever is under the hand that is touched. Then you invite your friend to put his or her two hands over any of the things that remain, and you touch one of them, eliminating whatever is under it. You cover two more, and your friend touches one of your hands, and so on, until all the things have been removed but one. That last one is the mustard.

"You've had a dozen choices," you say. "But by pure chance, the only thing left is the jar of mustard." You ask your friend to pick up the slip of paper and read aloud the prediction you wrote. It says: "Please pass me the mustard"!

THE SET-UP

There is nothing prearranged. You use whatever picnic things are handy. All you need is a pen and paper to write on.

WHAT YOU DO

Arrange any seven things in a spaced-apart row on the table. Decide which of them you want to be the one left after all the rest are eliminated. Depending on what happens to be on the table, you might decide the final thing is to be the cup, the can of cola, or the napkin. It can be whichever one you decide. That is the one you predict.

For example, let's say you decide it will be the mustard. Write your prediction for that, fold the paper, and put it where it will be in full view until the end. Now ask someone to join you in a "game of chance." Explain that you are going to take turns eliminating the things, one by one, until only one is left.

Put your two hands over any two things in the row, *except the mustard*. Ask your friend to touch either of your hands. Remove whatever is under the hand that is touched, and put it aside.

Then tell your friend to put his or her hands over any two things. If *neither* of the things chosen is the mustard, you can touch *either* hand and remove what is under it. But if your friend puts one hand over the mustard, you just touch the *other hand*, and eliminate what is under that.

Turn by turn, you continue the same thing. When it's your turn, you never cover the mustard; when it's your friend's turn, you always touch the hand that is not over the mustard. It looks like a fair choice each time, but there is never a chance to eliminate the mustard. At the end, that is necessarily the only thing left, and you ask your friend to open the paper and read aloud your prediction that seems to have come true by "pure chance."

OTHER WAYS TO DO IT

With All Sorts of Things

You can do this with almost any group of small objects that may be available at the moment wherever you happen to be: cards, coins, dice, poker chips, bills of various denominations, postage stamps, sticks and stones gathered up around a campfire, shells and pebbles from the beach, things from a desk drawer in the office, nuts and bolts from a home workshop, kitchen fruits and vegetables, canned goods, toys, or the miniature props of home games.

There must be an *odd number* of things set up at the start, so only one will remain after all the rest are eliminated. But they need not be all *different* things. For instance, you might want to do the trick with a handful of change from your pocket: three nickels, two dimes, two quarters.

If you decide one of the dimes is to be left at the end, you could write a prediction that says: "Thanks for leaving me a dime to make a phone call."

In this case, you would note the position of *one* of the two dimes as you laid the coins out in a row, and would simply make sure during the taking of turns and touching of hands to avoid eliminating that one.

Paper Castaways

You tear seven strips from an old newspaper, or use paper napkins or facial tissues. "Let's pretend that one of these isn't just a scrap of paper," you say. "It's a map giving directions to a buried treasure of pure gold. I'll mark a big 'X' on it, so we know which one is the map."

You mark an "X" on one of the strips with a pen, and then crumple that strip and each of the others into seven balls. Then you lay the balls out in a row, mixing them around to change their positions, being careful to keep track of where you finally place the one with the mark inside it.

Then you ask someone to take turns with you, eliminating the balls one by one. You pick up a ball in each hand, have your friend touch one of your hands, and you throw the crumpled ball of paper in that hand away, tossing it to the floor. You put the other ball back with the rest on the table. Your friend then picks up a ball in each hand, you touch one of them, and that ball is cast away. As before, you never give your friend a chance to eliminate the marked one.

"After all the choices you have made," you say at the end, "you finally have left only this one for me." Opening it out, you show everyone the "X" marked on the inside. "Thanks for giving me the map to the buried gold. . . . Now, if somebody has a shovel, I'll go dig up my treasure."

Headline Mentalist

For this one, you also tear seven pieces from an old newspaper. But as you open the paper to do that, secretly glance at one of the headlines and remember it. Then tear out that piece so the remembered headline is intact at the top.

You don't have to memorize the headline word for word. Just give it a quick glance, and remember in general what it is about. Crumple that strip of paper into a ball and put it on the table, and continue tearing out the other pieces and making a ball of each of those. Space out the crumpled balls of paper in a row, and keep track of the position of the one with the remembered headline.

Ask someone to help you, and say, "Just so nobody thinks you and I have arranged anything in advance, we'll do this so we reach a final choice entirely by chance." Pick up two of the paper balls, have your friend touch one of your hands, and throw that piece away. Then have him or her take one in each hand, touch one of his hands, let that piece be thrown away, and so on. When all the turns have been completed, point to the one that remains, which is the one with your remembered headline, and say, "That, then, is your final choice. Will you open it up and read it to yourself? But please don't say anything aloud."

You step aside, or turn your back and pretend to concentrate. "I get the impression that what you are reading has something to do with travel" (or whatever the headline happens to be about), you say. Then you go on to be more specific, naming some person or place in the headline, if you can.

CHAPTER 3

WITH A PACK OF CARDS

Twin Sets

HOW IT LOOKS

"I am about to make two predictions," you say, "and if they turn out to be even half right—then I'll probably be as surprised as you are."

You ask someone to shuffle thoroughly a borrowed pack of cards, and then you take the pack back and explain that you will look through it and remove two of the cards. You place those two cards face down on the table without showing them. "These will be my predictions."

Holding out the pack, you ask the person to cut the cards by lifting about half of them off the pack, and then putting those down on the table. You place the remaining half of the pack across the top of his half, and say, "I'll mark where you cut them. Remember, please, that the cards were as you shuffled them. . . . All right. Now let's look at them."

You turn over the top half of the pack and show, for example, that one of the cards cut to was the three of spades. Then you turn the first of your prediction cards face up, and show that it is the three of clubs. "The other black three," you say. "The matching twin to yours."

Now you turn over the top card of the bottom half of the pack, the other card where the pack was cut. It may be the king of hearts. When you show your second prediction card, it is the king of diamonds. "The other red king," you say. "Again the matching twin to yours. Two sets of twins!"

WHAT YOU DO

Take back the cards after someone has thoroughly shuffled them. Explain that you will look through the pack and remove two prediction cards.

Hold the pack facing you, and as you spread out the cards to look through them, secretly glance at the top and bottom cards. Remove the two *matching* cards of the same number and color, and put those face down on the table without showing them. (If the top and bottom cards are the nine of clubs and ace of diamonds, for instance, you would remove the nine of spades and ace of hearts.)

Square up the pack, and rest it face down on your outstretched right palm. Ask the person to lift off about half the pack and to put those cards down on the table. Immediately place your remaining half of the pack down *across* the top of his half, so the two halves lie criss-cross on the table, and say, "I'll mark where you cut them."

(That isn't *really* where he cut them, since all you have done is to place the original bottom half of the pack across the original top half, bringing what were the top and bottom cards of the pack together at the middle.)

It is psychologically important at this point to make some remark to distract your friend's attention momentarily so he won't realize the true position of the two halves of the pack, so you say, "Remember, please, that the cards are as you shuffled them. . . . All right. Now let's look at them."

Lift off what is now the top half of the criss-crossed pack, and turn that face up on the table. Point to the top card of that half, and say, "This is the first card you cut to. It happens to be the three of spades" (or whatever it is). Then turn your first prediction card face up. "Here is the other black three. The matching twin to yours."

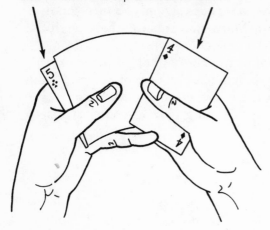

Look through the pack and remove the two that "match" the top and bottom cards

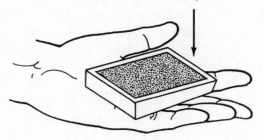

He takes some from top

Holding out pack to be cut

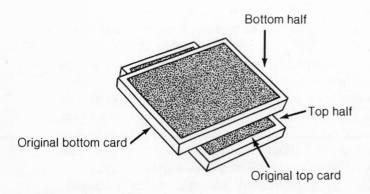

Bottom half

Top half

Original bottom card

Original top card

Cards on table—yours placed criss-cross on top of his

Put that card aside and point to the top card of the bottom half of the pack. "This is the second card that you cut to." Turn it face up. "This one happens to be the king of hearts [or whatever it is]." Lay your second prediction card face up beside it, and show that those two cards also match. "Again the matching twin to yours. Two sets of twins!"

OTHER WAYS TO DO IT

The Criss-Cross Force

This method of criss-crossing the two halves of the pack apparently to mark the place where someone cuts the cards is often used to force the choice of one or more cards you want the person to choose.

Just have the card or cards you want chosen secretly on the top or bottom of the pack at the start. If you start with the card on top, then, after the pack is criss-crossed as explained, it will be the first face-down card of the bottom half; if you start with the card on the bottom, it will be the bottom card of the upper half.

Whichever way you arrange it, finally lift off the top half of the crossed pack and have the person look at the card thought to be freely selected when the pack was first cut.

Anybody's Aces

You ask someone to cut freely a pack of cards that you place before him on the table, and the person immediately discovers that the pack has been cut to locate all four aces!

As simple as it is, this is a good opening trick for a card magic routine. There is an instant magical surprise to capture attention the moment you begin. The only set-up is to have two of the aces secretly on top of the pack, and the other two aces on the bottom.

Pick up the pack, and place it on the table in front of someone. "Please cut the pack in half," you say, and as the person does that, you point to a spot on the table so he or she will place that half down there. Immediately pick up the other half, and put that across the top of the first half, as if to mark the place where the cards were cut.

"Do you play cards a lot?" you jokingly ask. "Or is this just beginner's luck? You seem to have a gambler's touch."

Turn the top half of the pack face up, and show the first ace at the face of it. Slide that card off, and reveal the second ace beneath it. Drop that half pack on the table, and pick up the bottom half of the pack. Turn its top card face up to show the third ace. Deal off the next card, turn it up to show the final ace, and say, "All four aces. How lucky can you get?"

Small Fortune

Secretly have an eight on top of the pack, a two on the bottom, and twenty-eight cents in change in one of your left-hand pockets: two dimes, three pennies, and a nickel. (The money is in a left-hand pocket, so your right hand later will be free to handle the cards.)

Start the trick by placing the pack in front of someone. "I'll show you how you can tell somebody's fortune with cards," you say. "This is an easy first lesson. You're going to tell *my* fortune."

Ask the person to cut the pack by lifting about half the cards off the top, and point to where they are to be placed on the table. Lay the other half of the pack across the top of that half to mark "where you cut them."

Reach into your pocket, and bring out the handful of change without showing how much you have. Jingle the coins in your closed left hand, and say, "This is my fortune at the moment—such as it is."

Ask the person to turn over the top half of the pack and show the upturned card. "It happens to be a two," you say. Point to the top card of the other half, and ask that that one be turned face up. "And by chance, the other card you happened to choose is an eight. A two and an eight—twenty-eight."

Spread the coins from your hand out across the table and quickly count them aloud. "Exactly twenty-eight cents. . . . You've told my fortune!"

The Birthday Card

HOW IT LOOKS

"I don't know when your birthday is, but I think we should celebrate it right now," you tell someone, after asking that person to shuffle a pack of cards. "Do you mind choosing your own birthday card?"

You take back the pack, spread it between your hands, and invite the person to take any card and look at it without letting you see it, and then to return it to the middle of the pack. "I don't know what your choice was," you say. "But will you please remember it?"

After cutting the cards several times so that the chosen card is lost among the others, you stand the pack upright in a paper cup. The upper half of the pack sticks up above the top of the cup, making it seem obvious that there is no way in which you can manipulate the isolated pack.

"When *is* your birthday?" you ask. "Not the year you were born— just the month and the day." The person may answer, for instance, "January ninth."

You spell out the month and the day, taking one card from the pack for each letter, and dropping them singly face down on the table. "J-A-N-U-A-R-Y . . . N-I-N-T-H." When you have finished spelling out the month and day, you say, "If the astrological signs are right, your birth date may have had a strong influence on these cards. Which card did you first choose from the pack as your own personal birthday card?"

The person says, for instance, "The five of spades." You ask that he or she turn over the last card drawn from the cup and dropped on the table. It is the person's chosen "birthday card," the five of spades.

THE SET-UP

Most paper and plastic cups in everyday use have tapering sides; they are broad at the top and narrower at the bottom. They will hold an upright pack with the top half of the cards extending above the cup rim, but with the bottom end of the pack kept from going all the way down to the bottom of the cup by the tapering sides.

You can do the trick wherever a cup of that kind is available. Have it on your table at the start.

WHAT YOU DO

Have someone shuffle the cards, and then take them back and spread the pack face down between your hands. Ask the person to remove any card as his or her chosen "birthday card," and to look at it without letting you see it. While the person is doing that, close up the pack and hold it in your left hand, with your thumb at the left side edge and fingers up around the opposite side edge.

Lift off about half the pack with your right hand, and hold out the remainder with your left hand so the person can put his or her card back on top of those. Bring your right hand down over the left one to replace that half of the pack. *But just as your hands come together,* secretly bend in the tip of your left little finger so that the cards from the right hand go

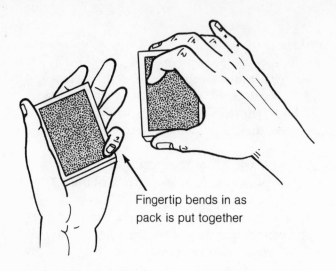

Fingertip bends in as
pack is put together

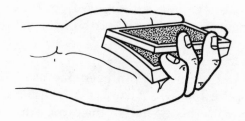

Little finger holds "break" between halves

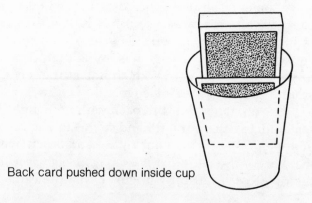

Back card pushed down inside cup

down on top of the fingertip. Press your left thumb lightly on top of the pack to keep its front edges closed.

This looks as if you simply put the halves of the pack back together, with the chosen card buried in the middle. But your little finger acts as a place mark, holding a "break" at the rear edge that cannot be seen from the front. The chosen card is right beneath the space held open by your little finger.

What you seem to do next is to cut the pack several times so that the chosen card is well lost among the others. With your right hand, lift off about half the cards that are above the "break," and put them down on the table. Then lift off all the remaining cards above the "break," and put those down on top of the first batch on the table. Finally put the rest of the pack down on top of the others. This leaves the chosen card on top of the pack.

Pick up the pack with your right hand. Hold it upright, with the face to the front. Put it down inside the cup, and as you do that, just push the back card *all the way down to the bottom of the cup* with your thumb. Secretly sliding that back card down behind the pack slightly buckles its side edges, so it is held in place and kept down out of the way. The top edge of that back card (the chosen card) is now about an inch below the top edge of the pack inside the cup.

Leave the cup standing on the table with the upright pack in it, and ask the person the month and day he or she was born. When you have the answer, bring your right hand to the top of the pack. Pull out the card that is second from the back, and drop it face down on the table as you start to spell aloud. (This is easy to do without fumbling, because the top end of the pack is well above the pushed-down back card.)

Continue to remove one card for each letter, dropping them singly to the table. As you spell the last letter of the person's birth date, pull out the pushed-down back card and drop that on top of the others. Ask the person to name the chosen card, and then have him or her turn over that last one and discover it is the "birthday card."

OTHER WAYS TO DO IT

With a Glass Instead of a Cup

If there are no paper or plastic cups handy, you may find a drinking glass with tapered sides that is big enough to hold a pack of cards. But if you use a transparent glass, keep it held in your left hand instead of standing it on the table, with your fingers around the bottom front of the glass so those watching can't look through it and see the pushed-down card.

Under Your Spell

Since the cup allows you to pull out a chosen card whenever you wish, you can spell out any combination of words or letters to produce it without sleight of hand or elaborately prearranging the cards in the pack.

Just have someone choose a card and return it to the pack. Secretly bring the card to the top, and push it down while putting the pack into the cup, as explained previously. Then ask the person to call out the name of the chosen card. As soon as this is done, you can immediately spell it, removing one card for each letter. Pull out the chosen card as you spell the last letter.

You can spell out the name of a club, sports team or other group, a business organization or its product, the name of the person who chose the card, or even find the card on the last letter of his or her grandmother's middle name if it is slowly spelled aloud as you draw cards from the pack.

The Cup Force

The cup also can be used to force the choice of a card. Simply have the card you want someone to choose on top of the pack at the start. Explain that you want to "isolate the cards" so they will be completely out of your hands.

Put the pack into the cup, secretly pushing down that back card, and ask the person to call out any number from one to twenty—or the last two digits of his or her social security, telephone, or license plate number.

Move the cards one at a time from the back to the front of the pack until you reach the called number, or pull them singly from the back and drop them to the table as you count.

If you ask to have a two-digit number called, count out the first digit, and then the second. Don't combine the two, or you may be faced with counting out an impossibly large number of cards, such as fifty-seven or ninety-nine.

The Two Fastest Tricks in the World

HOW IT LOOKS

You borrow a pack of cards, and tell the person you borrowed them from that you want a card chosen entirely by chance. You ask the person to lift about half the cards off the top, turn the cards over face up, and drop them back on the pack. He or she then looks at the first face-down card, puts it back, and thoroughly shuffles the pack.

"I'll show you the fastest card trick in the world," you say, as you put the shuffled pack into your jacket pocket and remove your hand. You ask the person to call out the name of the chosen card. The instant you hear it, you plunge your hand back into your pocket and pull out the chosen card.

After showing it, you say, "We won't need this one anymore. . . . Do you mind if I get rid of it?" Keeping its face toward the person all the while, you deliberately tear the card in half, put the pieces together, and tear them in half again. You openly put the torn pieces into your pants or skirt pocket, then show your hand is empty, and take the pack from your jacket pocket to place that on the table.

"If you're worried because I ruined your pack of cards—don't be," you say, "because I'm about to show you the *second* fastest trick in the world."

You hold your hand in front of your pants or skirt pocket. "Four little pieces in my pocket." You snap your fingers four times. "And now there are none." Pulling the pocket lining inside out, you show the pocket is empty. "The pieces have flown back into the pack. . . . And on the way, they have pulled themselves all together again."

You flip the pack over on the table, spread out the face-up cards, and remove the chosen one the person saw you tear into bits, now completely restored!

THE SET-UP

Just have any card from an old pack of your own in your empty right-hand jacket pocket. Stand it on *end*, face *outward*, and remember which card it is. Your right pants or skirt pocket should be empty.

You lift off small packet

Then turn them face up and drop them back on top

Someone lifts off half the pack— then turns them over and puts them back on top

First face-down card— was on top at start

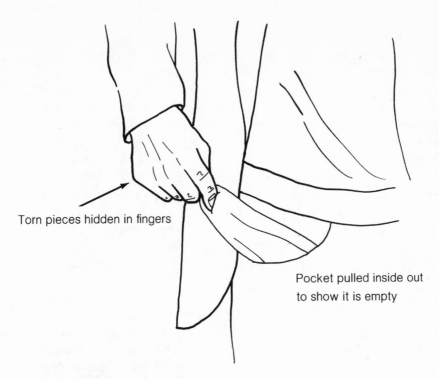

Torn pieces hidden in fingers

Pocket pulled inside out
to show it is empty

WHAT YOU DO

Borrow the pack, and say you want to make sure there is no joker in it. Look through the cards as if searching for a joker, but really look for the card that matches the extra one in your pocket. Lift off all the cards behind the one that matches the card you have hidden, put those at the face of the pack to leave the matching one on top, and quickly run through the pack again. If there is a joker, remove it and place it aside; otherwise say, "Just the fifty-two cards—no joker."

Square up the pack, hold it face down, and explain to the person you borrowed it from that you want a card chosen entirely at random. You demonstrate what you want the person to do by lifting a small packet of cards (about a dozen) off the pack, turning them face up, and dropping them back on top.

Leaving the cards as they are, with your packet turned face up, hold out the pack in your left hand and say, "Just lift about half the cards off the pack, turn the batch face up, and drop them back on top."

When that has been done, you spread the pack out in your hands until you come to the first face-down card, and say, "Here's the one you cut to entirely by chance. Will you take it and look at it, please, without letting me see it?" While the person is looking at that card, turn all the cards face down, and then hand him or her the pack. Ask the person to put his or her card back anywhere, and to shuffle the pack thoroughly.

(You have forced the person to choose what originally was the top card of the pack, the one that matches the extra card in your pocket. The double turnover of face-up cards looks convincingly fair, but it leaves the original top card as the first one that is face down beneath the batch the person turned face up.)

Take back the shuffled pack, put it lengthwise into your jacket pocket, and remove your hand. Turn your right side toward those watching, and ask the person to call out the name of the chosen card. Thrust your hand into your pocket, take the extra matching card (the only one standing upright) by its top edge, and immediately bring it out. Hold it close to you, and be careful to keep its back toward you as you face front again. (Its back is different, of course, from the backs of the borrowed pack.)

Show it for a moment, and then say, "We won't need this one any more. . . . Do you mind if I get rid of it?" Bring your left hand to the top edge of the card, hold the card between the fingers of both hands, and slowly tear it in half from top to bottom, tearing it *toward* you. Be careful again to avoid revealing its back as you put the torn halves together, turn them sidewise, and tear through both.

Hold the pieces between your right thumb and first finger, and openly put them into the bottom of your pants or skirt pocket. Show your hand is empty as you bring it out, then reach into your jacket pocket, take out the pack of cards, and place that face down at the far left of the table. "If you're worried because I ruined your pack of cards— don't be," you say, "because I'm about to show you the second fastest trick in the world."

Bring your right hand down in front of your pants or skirt pocket, and say, "Four little pieces in my pocket." Snap your fingers four times. "And now there are none."

Put your hand into the pocket. With your thumb, quickly slide the torn pieces into your three lower fingers, closing those fingers tightly around the pieces to hide them, and grip the bottom of the pocket lining between your thumb and first finger. Pull the pocket inside out, still holding it between your finger and thumb, with the back of the hand naturally toward those watching, the pieces concealed in your fingers.

Hold the pocket pulled out that way for a moment, shake it gently to indicate that it is empty, and then push the pocket back in, leaving the pieces in it as you remove your hand.

"The pieces have flown back into the pack," you say, as you reach out to the table and flip the pack over, face up. Spread the cards out across the table, locate the person's matching chosen card, slide it out of the spread, and hold it up to show it completely restored. "And on the way, they have pulled themselves all together again!"

OTHER WAYS TO DO IT

The Deuce You Say

This amusing trick explains a way to use the double turnover of batches of cards on top of a pack to force the selection of two different cards, each apparently chosen by chance. Set it up by having the two of clubs and two of spades secretly on top of the pack.

Start by telling someone you want him or her to choose a card entirely by chance, and show what you want done by lifting a small batch of cards off the top, turning them over face up, and dropping them back on the pack.

Leave those cards as they are, hold out the pack on your left hand, and ask the person to lift off about half the cards and to turn them over face up and then drop them back on top. When that has been done, spread the pack between your hands until you come to the first face-down card (the first of the two that originally were stacked on top).

"That's where you happened to cut the cards by chance," you say. Take all the face-up cards in your right hand, turn them face down, and put them underneath the pack at the bottom. Point to the top card, and say, "Will you take your card—but don't look at it yet. Just place it face down on the table. . . . Now I'll do the same thing, and let's see what card chance brings to me."

Lift a small batch of cards off the top, turn them over face up, and drop them back on the pack. Then lift off about half the pack, turn those cards over face up, and drop them back on top. As before, spread the pack in your hands until you come to the first face-down card, and say, "There's mine."

Take all the face-up cards in your right hand, turn them face down, and put them under the pack at the bottom. Remove the top card (the second of the two that originally were stacked on top) and place it face down on the table next to the first.

Ask the person to turn his or her card face up and look at it. "The two of spades," you say. "The black deuce." Then bend up the back end of your card far enough to glance at it. Shake your head, and say, "That's quite a coincidence. Mine is a black card, too." Flip your card over, face up, next to the other one. "And the deuce of it is—mine's a *two*, too."

Using the Pocket Dodge with Coins

The way the pocket was used to vanish the torn pieces of a card is a useful dodge to remember when you are doing other impromptu tricks with any small object that can be concealed in your fingers as you pull the pocket inside out. With it you can make such things as a coin, a key, or a pair of dice seem to appear, disappear, or change into something else.

To magically introduce some routine with a coin, for instance, you can use the pocket to help you seem to pluck the coin out of the air.

Have the coin in your right-hand pants or skirt pocket, and start by reaching into that pocket. Secretly get the coin hidden in your fingers, pull the pocket inside out to show it is empty, as explained previously, and hold the lining pulled out as you say, "I seem to have run out of money. Doesn't everybody these days?"

Push the pocket back in, but keep the coin hidden in your fingers as you take your hand out of the pocket again and let the hand fall to your side for a moment. "I wish I were *really* a magician who could pull money out of the air whenever I wanted it," you say. Sweep your hand up into the air, and with your thumb push the coin up into view at your fingertips, as though catching it. "Just like that!"

Coin through Your Body

By having two look-alike coins, one in each pocket, you can make a coin seem to pass invisibly "through your body" from pocket to pocket.

Start by taking the coin out of the right-hand pocket. Show the coin, put it back into the pocket, and bring your hand out and show it is empty.

Then put your left hand into your left pocket, get that coin hidden in your fingers, and pull the pocket inside out, holding it out to show it is empty. As you push the lining back in, leave the coin in the pocket.

Snap your fingers first in front of the right pocket, and then the left one. Put your right hand into your right-hand pocket, get the coin hidden in your fingers, and pull the pocket inside out to show that the coin has vanished. Push that pocket in, leaving the coin there, and remove your hand.

Reach into your other pocket with your left hand, and bring out the coin that seems to have passed "through your body" from pocket to pocket.

Scrambled Aces

HOW IT LOOKS

"Once somebody asked an old Mississippi riverboat gambler what he would like for breakfast, and he said, 'Make mine scrambled aces!'" you say. "So the cook scrambled up a whole pack of cards."

You lift small batches of cards off the top of the pack in your hand, turning each batch over as you drop it back on top of the pack. "Face up. . . . Face down. . . . Face up. . . . Face down." Spreading out the pack in your hands, you show the mixed cards. "Some are face up and some face down." To further mix them, you divide the pack and put the halves back together, one half face up and one half face down. "Finally the cook flipped the whole pack over four times." You turn the entire pack over and over, as you count, "One . . . two . . . three . . . four."

Then you quickly spread the cards out across the table in a long overlapping row. "But when he spread the cards out on the gambler's table, they were *all face up again*—except for these." All the cards have turned face up, except for four that are face down in the center. You turn those four cards over and show that they are the aces. "One . . . two . . . three . . . four. The scrambled aces!"

THE SET-UP

Secretly have the four aces stacked *face up* together at the bottom of the *face-down* pack.

WHAT YOU DO

Hold the pack squared in your left hand. With your right hand, lift a batch of about half a dozen cards off the top. Turn them over face up, drop them back on the pack, and say, "Face up."

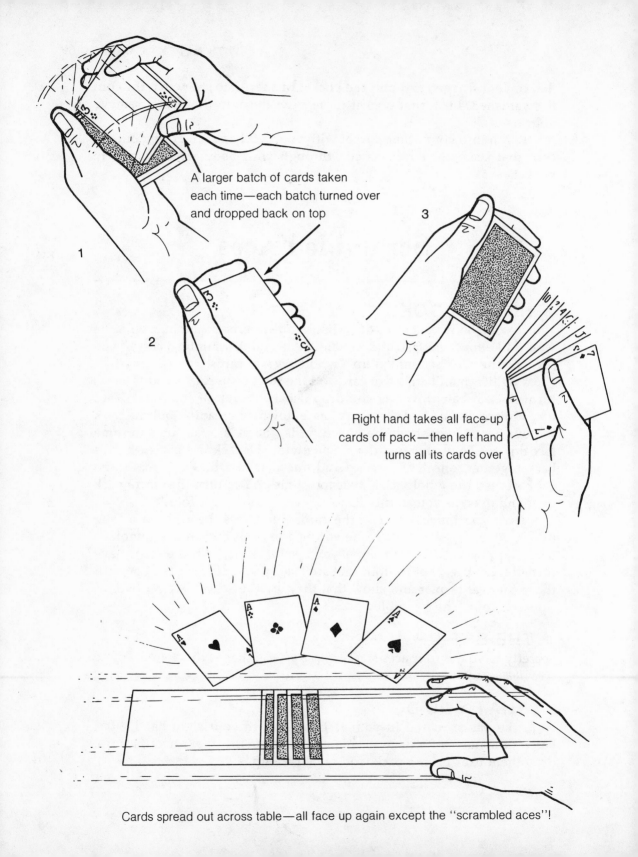

A larger batch of cards taken each time—each batch turned over and dropped back on top

1

2

3

Right hand takes all face-up cards off pack—then left hand turns all its cards over

Cards spread out across table—all face up again except the "scrambled aces"!

Now lift about one-quarter of the pack off the top (including the first batch), turn these cards over, drop them back on the pack, and say, "Face down."

Next lift about half the pack off the top, turn these cards over, drop them back, and say, "Face up." Then lift off three-quarters of the pack, turn these cards over, drop them back, and say, "Face down."

These turnings really leave *all* the cards at the top of the pack face up, and *all* the cards in the lower half face down, except for the face-up aces hidden at the bottom.

Spread the cards in your hands, being careful not to expose the aces at the bottom. Divide the pack, and take all the face-up cards from the top in your right hand. Show the face-down cards in the left hand. Then openly turn those left-hand cards over, which brings the aces, now face down, to the top. Drop the face-up cards from the right hand on top of what seem to be the face-down cards in the left hand, and say, "Some face up, and some face down."

At this point, all the cards are really face up except for the face-down aces in the center, but you don't reveal them yet. "Finally the cook flipped the whole pack over four times," you say, turning the pack over, end for end, as you count, "One . . . two . . . three . . . four."

Then you spread the cards across the table in an overlapping row to show they have all turned face up once more, except for the four. You point to those, slide them out of the spread, and turn them over. "One . . . two . . . three . . . four. The scrambled aces!"

OTHER WAYS TO DO IT

Triple Mix Aces

In this version, the pack is divided into three piles on the table, two face up and one face down. Two piles are mixed face to face, and then all three piles are mixed, with some of the cards facing up and others facing down. But at the end, all the cards have turned face down, and the four aces appear face up among them.

Start as before with the four aces secretly stacked face up on the bottom of the face-down pack. Hold the pack squared in your left hand. With the right hand, lift about one-third of the cards off the top, and put

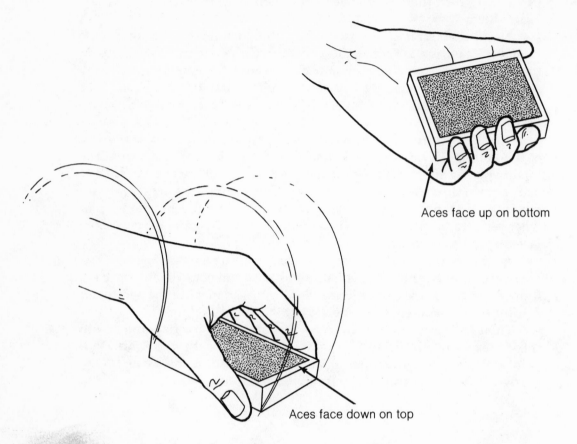

Aces face up on bottom

Aces face down on top

Left hand just turns palm down—which secretly turns over its cards

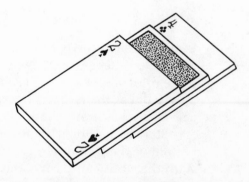

The sandwiched piles on table

them in a pile on the table. Then lift off another one-third of the cards, and put those beside the first pile on the table.

Now reach out with your right hand, and turn each of those two piles *face up*. At the same time, while attention is on your right hand, just turn your left hand over palm downward, which secretly turns over the cards it is holding. (The cards still look face down, as they were, but now are really face up, except for the face-down aces on top.)

Place those cards from your left hand on either of the face-up piles on the table so they overlap the bottom end of that pile, leaving about half the face-up pile showing beneath them. Point to each of the two overlapping piles, and say, "Face up . . . face down."

Push those two piles together, square them up, and say, "Face to face." Turn the piles over together, end for end, and then turn them over again, to show that cards are face down on both sides. (Turning them over twice brings the face-down aces back to the top, and leaves all the others face up beneath them.)

Lift about half the cards off the top of the pushed-together piles, and place them on the face-up pile that you haven't used so far, overlapping them so part of that face-up pile extends beneath them. Then place the rest of the cards on top, again overlapping so part of the middle pile extends beneath them. Point to each of the three overlapping parts of the pack, and say, "Face up. . . . Face down. . . . Face up."

Push the three stepped-out parts together, and square up the pack. Turn the entire pack over, end for end, *three times*. Quickly spread the cards out across the table in a long overlapping row to show that they have all turned themselves face down again—and that the four aces have appeared face up at the center!

The Ghost Card

HOW IT LOOKS

You invite a friend to help you, and ask him or her to stand beside you. "Let's pretend we're a couple of ghosts at a party the ghosts are having in an old deserted house," you say. "Being ghosts, we're invisible, of course—so we'll use an invisible pack of cards. I have them in my pocket."

You reach into your pocket, and bring out your empty hand as if you were holding a pack of cards. "Here they are. First, I'll shuffle them thoroughly." You pretend to shuffle them and then to spread them out between your hands, and you ask the person to choose any card from the invisible pack. "Just take it out, look at it without letting me see it, and put it back in the pack," you say. "Please keep that card in mind. You won't forget it, will you?"

After your friend has pretended to take a card and return it, you explain, "I'll shuffle the cards again so your card is well lost among the others." You go through the motions of shuffling. "Now I'll glance through the pack just once, and take out one card and put that in my pocket." Acting it out, you remove an imaginary card from the invisible pack, put your empty hand into your pocket as if to leave it there, and bring your hand out.

"Will you please tell everyone the name of the one card you have in mind?" you say. "What was your card?"

Your friend may answer, "The three of spades."

You reach into your pocket and take out one *real* card. Holding it up, you show those watching that it *is* the three of spades! "Thank you for helping me fool all the other ghosts," you tell your friend. "Let's keep it a secret that we went out haunting together."

THE SET-UP

This is a trick to do before a fairly large group. The one friend who acts as your helper will discover how it was done, but the patter is planned to encourage him or her to keep the secret and to play along with you to enjoy the fun of fooling the others.

Ahead of time, take one card from a pack of your own. Let's say it's the three of spades. From a business card or index card, cut out a one-inch square of thin blank cardboard. With a black marking pen, print a big number 3 and a spade symbol on it.

Take a two-inch strip of transparent tape, stick the center of it across the back of the little piece of cardboard, then fasten the two ends of tape together and flatten it. This leaves a sticky side of the tape outward, so that you can later secretly attach the piece of cardboard to the palm of your hand. Turn the piece of cardboard so the markings face you, and bend the two tiny tips of the top corners down toward the front, so that you will be able to tell by feeling that the top end is up.

Carry the matching playing card in the empty right-hand pocket of your jacket with the face of the card toward your body. Put the card you

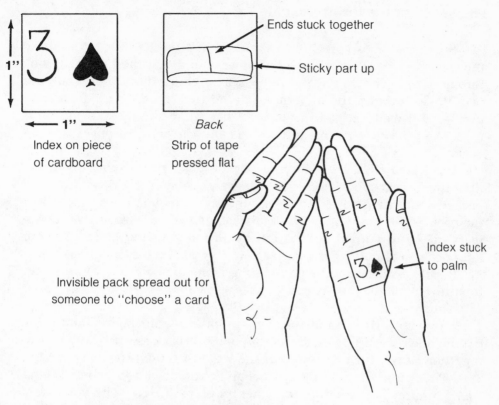

1"

1"

Index on piece
of cardboard

Back
Strip of tape
pressed flat

Ends stuck together

Sticky part up

Index stuck
to palm

Invisible pack spread out for
someone to "choose" a card

have cut and indexed down behind it, with its sticky side toward the outside of the pocket.

WHAT YOU DO

Invite someone from the group to help you. Stand so that he or she is at your left side. Talk about the ghosts and the invisible pack of cards. Reach into your pocket with your right hand. Feel for the bent corners so you know the index card is top end up, and stick it firmly to the palm of your hand, near the base of the middle fingers.

Bring your hand out, with its back toward those watching, and hold up the imaginary pack to show it. Pretend to shuffle the cards and then to spread them out so your friend can pretend to choose one. Turn toward your friend, with your hands apart as though holding the spread pack, and say, " Just take it out, look at it without letting me see it, and put it back in the pack."

Tilt your right hand up slightly, so your friend has a clear view of the index card fastened to the palm of it. Keep the hand held that way, and say, "Just keep that card in mind." Look up at your friend, smile, and ask, "You won't forget it, will you?"

Face forward as you explain that you will shuffle the pack again so the chosen card is "lost among the others," and that then you will look through the pack just once to remove a single card and put it in your pocket. Go through the motions of doing that, holding the imaginary pack as if it were fanned in your left hand and the faces of the cards were toward you. Pretend to take out one card and to put it in your pocket.

With your right hand in your pocket, push your thumb under the little index card so it comes free from your palm. Let it drop into your pocket, and bring your hand out again. Say, "We won't need the rest of the pack, so I'll put that away." Make believe you are closing the imaginary pack still fanned in your left hand. Put your left hand into your left pocket as if putting the pack away, and take that hand out again.

"Will you please tell everyone the name of the one card you have in mind?" you ask your friend. "What was your chosen card?"

Your friend answers, "The three of spades."

Show your right hand is empty, reach into your pocket, and bring out the one *real* card. Hold the card up with its back toward those watching, then slowly turn it around to show that it *is* the three of spades!

"Thank you for helping me fool all the other ghosts," you tell your friend, indirectly thanking him or her for playing along with you to fool the others who are watching. "Let's keep it a secret that we went out haunting together."

OTHER WAYS TO DO IT

Gaze into My Crystal Ball

You ask to borrow a pack of cards and a drinking glass, and invite someone from the group to help you. "I'll look through these cards and choose just one of them without letting you see it," you explain, "and I'll put that card in my pocket."

You spread the faces of the cards toward you, select one without showing it, and put it in your pocket. "Now what I want you to do is to read my mind," you say. "If I had a crystal ball, I'd ask you to gaze into that. But since we don't have a crystal ball—we'll just use this glass to help you concentrate your thoughts."

Picking up the glass, you hold it in front of the person, and ask him to clear his mind of all other thoughts and try to "form a mental vision

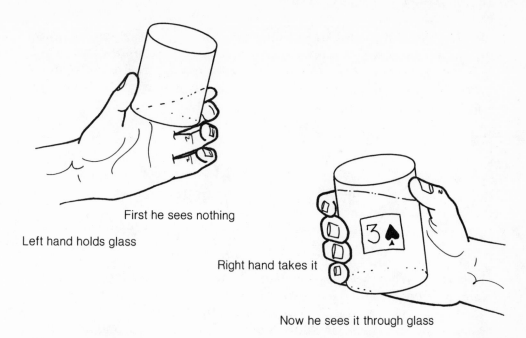

First he sees nothing

Left hand holds glass

Right hand takes it

Now he sees it through glass

of just one card." He doesn't see anything at first, so you hold the glass closer and tell him to concentrate harder. You ask, "Has one card come to your mind? Which card is it?"

The person answers, "The three of spades."

You reach into your pocket, take out the one card you removed from the pack, and show everybody it *is* the three of spades!

All you need in your pocket for this one is the little square of cardboard with sticky tape on its back, marked with a big index of the three of spades (or any other card you wish).

When you look through the borrowed pack at the start of the trick, just remove the card matching the one you have made, without showing it, and put it in your pocket. While your hand is in the pocket, secretly stick the small hand-marked index to your palm, as explained. Bring your hand out with its back toward those watching, and pick up the glass from the table.

Transfer the glass to your left hand, let your right hand fall to your side, and hold up the glass so the person can gaze into it. He doesn't see anything, so you take the glass again with your right hand around the front of it, remove your left hand, and hold the glass closer to him as you tell him to concentrate harder. The person now can see the big three of spades index through the glass.

Ask him to name the one card he has in mind and then put the glass on the table and reach into your pocket. Thumb off the little cardboard index, drop it into your pocket, and bring out the real card to show everybody that the person did have a "mental vision" of the one card you removed from the pack.

Prize Surprise

HOW IT LOOKS

"Will you join me in a guessing game?" you ask, as you take an envelope from your pocket and show that it is sealed and taped. "Just to make it interesting, I've sealed a little prize inside this envelope."

You put the envelope aside, pick up a pack of cards, and ask someone to choose one card. After the person has looked at the card and returned it to the pack, you mix the cards and then have him divide the pack in two. You place the envelope on top of one half of the pack, and put the rest of the pack on top of the envelope, so the envelope is sandwiched between the two halves.

"Now I want you to guess whether the card you chose is in the upper half or in the lower half of the pack," you say. Taking whichever half is picked, you show the person each of the cards in that half, but the chosen card is not among them. "I'm afraid your guess was wrong," you say. "But I'll give you a second chance. If it wasn't in that half, then it must be in this other half. Just tell me when you see your card."

You show each of the cards in the other half of the pack, but the chosen card still is not among them. "It seems to have vanished completely from the entire pack," you say. "What card *did* you choose?"

The person may answer that it was the seven of spades. You pick up the sealed envelope, tear one end off it, and reach down inside. "Here's the prize you might have won," you say, as you pull the missing card out of the envelope. "It's your own lost card—the seven of spades!"

THE SET-UP

You will need an empty envelope and a roll of transparent tape. Although the envelope flap is genuinely sealed, three short strips of tape are used, and the center strip is attached with its sticky side up.

When the envelope is sandwiched between the two halves of the pack, it secretly goes on top of the chosen card, which sticks to the back of the envelope because of the sticky tape. At the end of the trick, you pull the card up from behind the torn-open envelope in a way that looks as if you are pulling it out from inside.

Wet the flap and seal the empty envelope. Take a strip of tape about an inch and a half long and turn it *sticky side up*. To the upper right end of that, attach a longer strip of tape at an upward slant, with its *sticky side down*. Lay the first piece horizontally across the bottom point at the center of the flap, and fasten the attached second strip up along the right edge of the flap.

Finally attach one end of a third strip, *sticky side down*, to the top left corner of the first one at an upward slant, and fasten the rest of that third strip up along the left edge of the flap. The tape should not extend all the way up to the top corners of the envelope, because that would make it difficult to tear the envelope open quickly.

Fixed that way, the sticky part of the tape at the center is well disguised. You can carry the envelope in a jacket pocket or purse until you are ready to borrow a pack of cards and do the trick. The fact that the pack is borrowed makes it obvious that there are no duplicate cards involved.

(If you are showing the trick to a fairly large group, you may want to have the envelope sealed with bright-colored plastic tape, instead of the colorless transparent, for greater visibility.)

WHAT YOU DO

Invite your viewers to join you in a guessing game. Take out the envelope, show both sides of it, hold it with taped back toward those watching, and explain that you have sealed "a little prize" inside it to make the game interesting. Put the envelope aside, face up on the table.

Spread the cards in your hands and ask someone to choose one card, look at the card, and show it to the others without letting you see it. When the card is returned, secretly bring it to the top of the pack in the way that was explained earlier in this chapter in *The Birthday Card* trick. (This looks as if you are mixing the cards as you cut the pack several times and put it face down on the table.)

"Will you please divide the pack in two," you say. "Just take about half the cards and put them over here." Touch your fingertip to the table to indicate where the person is to put the half he cuts off the pack.

When that has been done, place the center of the face-up envelope vertically on top of the cards the person has removed from the pack. This

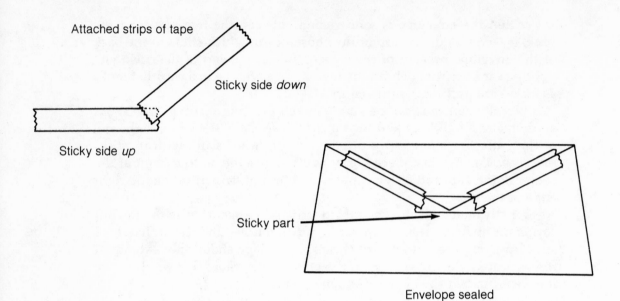

Attached strips of tape

Sticky side *down*

Sticky side *up*

Sticky part

Envelope sealed

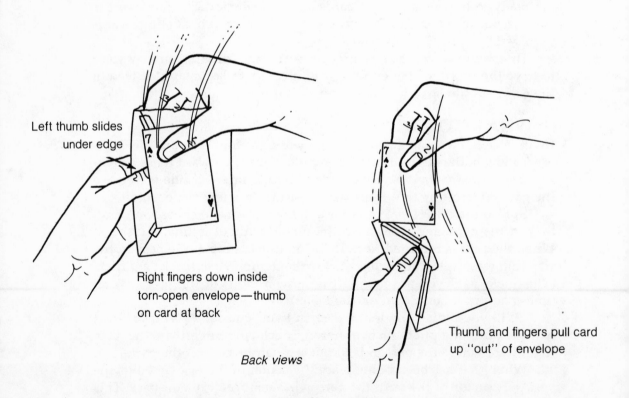

Left thumb slides
under edge

Right fingers down inside
torn-open envelope—thumb
on card at back

Back views

Thumb and fingers pull card
up "out" of envelope

brings the sticky tape at the back of the envelope against the chosen card that is beneath it. Then put the rest of the pack on top of the envelope, so the envelope is sandwiched between the two halves. As you do that, press down slightly on top of the pack, to make sure the chosen card sticks to the sandwiched envelope.

"Now I want you to guess whether the card you chose is in the upper half or the lower half of the pack," you say. "Which half do you guess?"

Whatever the answer, take the end of the envelope between your right thumb and fingers. Holding it as though it were a tray, lift off the envelope and the half-pack that is on top of it, and put it on the table next to the remaining half of the pack. (The chosen card, stuck to the tape, is now under the envelope on the table.)

Pick up whichever half of the pack the person has guessed the card might be in, and ask him to tell you when the chosen card appears as you deal the cards out face up, one at a time.

"You didn't see your card?" you ask, when you have finished showing them. "I'm afraid your guess was wrong. But I'll give you a second chance. If it wasn't in that half of the pack, then it must be in this half." Pick up the other half, turn it face up, and deal those cards out, one at a time. "Just tell me when you see your card."

The person still doesn't see it, and you say, "It seems to have vanished completely from the entire pack. What card *did* you choose?" Repeat aloud whatever card is named, so everybody knows which one it was—for instance, "The seven of spades?"

Take the bottom right end of the envelope between your right first finger and thumb. Tilt the envelope vertically upright, with its back toward you. Place your left hand around the front of it, and hold it with your fingers across to the right edge, with your thumb at the back *behind* the left edge. With your right hand, tear off the top end of the envelope. Squeeze the sides with your left hand to buckle it wide open at the top.

Put your right fingers down *inside* the top of the envelope as far as they will go, sliding your right thumb down *behind* it to bring the tip of that thumb down over the top end of the card hidden at the back. At the same time, slide the tip of your *left* thumb up under the left edge of the card, which lifts it slightly and frees it from the tape.

"Here's the prize you might have won," you say. Quickly pull the card straight up between your right thumb and fingers as you draw your fingers up out of the envelope. "It's your own lost card—the seven of spades!"

Sealed Prophecy

An empty envelope sealed in the same way, with a sticky strip on the back flap, can be used for this very simple and direct "prediction" trick. Have the envelope in the right pocket of your jacket, standing on end with its back toward your body.

Borrow a pack of cards, have one chosen by one of your friends, secretly bring it to the top, and put the pack face down on the table. "Hours ago," you say, "I made a prediction and placed a sealed envelope in my pocket."

With your right hand, reach into your pocket, take the top end of the envelope between your thumb and first finger, and bring the envelope out to show it. Turn your hand so everyone can see the back flap is sealed with tape, and then hold the envelope flat and face up as you bring your hand down to the pack of cards on the table and *drop* the envelope on top of the pack.

Leave the envelope lying there for a moment, centered upon the chosen card that secretly was brought to the top of the pack. "I've given you fifty-two possible choices," you say. "Fifty-two cards. Neither of us could know which of those choices you would make."

Pick up the envelope by placing your four right fingertips on top of it and your thumb under the end that is toward you. Press down with your fingertips so the card sticks to the tape. As you lift the envelope away, tilt it up with its back toward you, and then bring your left hand around the front of it, to hold it as previously explained.

Tear off the top end of the envelope, glance at the face of the card stuck to the back of it, and say: "My prediction was that you would choose the four of hearts [or whatever that card is] . . . and that the very card you chose would somehow vanish from the pack and appear inside this envelope."

Put your right fingers down inside the envelope and quickly pull the card up "out" of it. Turn the card around to show its face, and ask, "Was this the choice you made?"

MIXING PLEASURE WITH BUSINESS

◄—►

Magic Printing

HOW IT LOOKS

"Have you seen these new *onset* business cards?" you ask, as you take out a card and show it. "They're called that because at the *onset* there's no *offset*—nothing printed on them. They're just blank cards." You turn the card over to show that it is blank on both sides. "That way, you can print them as you need them, and keep all the information on them up to date."

You place the blank card on your hand, turn your hand over with your fingers closed around it, and push the card through from side to side with your thumb. The card remains blank the first two times you do that, but when you slowly push it through your hand a third time, it comes out fully printed as a regular business card!

"There it is," you say, as you give the card to someone to keep. "Onset printing—it works like magic."

THE SET-UP

Have a small stack of printed business cards, blank sides up, in your card case or wallet.

WHAT YOU DO

Remove one of the cards, keeping it flat so as not to reveal the printed underside, and put the rest of them away. Hold the card, blank side up, in your right palm, lying vertically on the hand, with your fingers curled up over the left long edge and the pad of your thumb against the right long edge.

What you seem to do now is to show that both sides of the card are blank by turning your hand over, back upward, from right to left. But as you begin to turn your hand over, grip the left edge of the card with your fingers. Slide your thumb *under* the card, press the tip of the thumb up against the center of the card, and just continue to turn the hand over until it is back upward, with the card held out between your thumb and fingers.

This is a simple and deceptive move, and very easy to do. The card isn't really turned over; only your hand is turned over, and the card remains blank side up with the printing still hidden on its underside. (Try it a few times as you watch yourself in a mirror, and you will see how convincing the turnover looks.)

Now hold your left palm out in front of you. Lay the card lengthwise, blank side up, across the tips of your left fingers. Turn your left hand over, palm down, closing your fingers up against your hand to hold the card. Your closing fingers automatically turn the card over as you turn your hand, so that it is still blank side up inside your hand.

With your closed hand back upward, push your left thumb against the right end of the card, pushing the card through your hand until it is halfway out the left side. Take the emerging "blank" card with your right thumb and first finger.

Draw the card all the way out of your left hand, and then turn the empty left hand palm upward again. Repeat the same thing, by placing the card across your fingertips and closing your hand as you turn it over to push the card through a second time.

The card has twice passed through your hand, and both times has come out blank. Once more, turn your left hand palm upward. But this

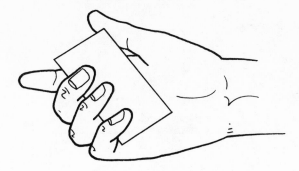

1 Card lies blank side up
on right palm—printing
hidden on underside

2 As you start to turn hand
over thumb pushes up
under card

3 Hand turned over back upward—
card still blank side up

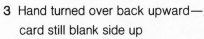

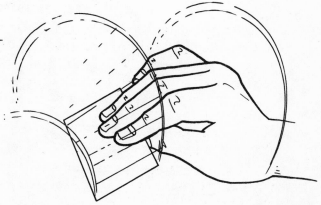

(*continued on next page*)

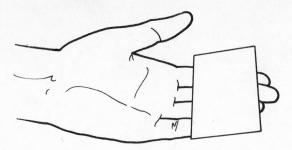

Card laid across left fingertips

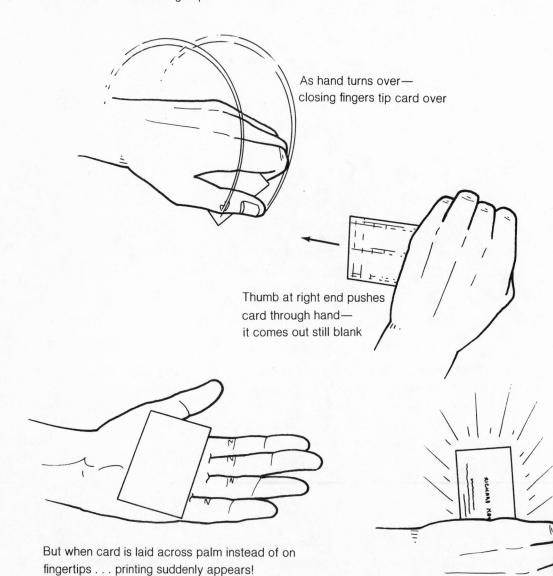

As hand turns over—
closing fingers tip card over

Thumb at right end pushes
card through hand—
it comes out still blank

But when card is laid across palm instead of on
fingertips . . . printing suddenly appears!

time, instead of laying the card across your fingertips, lay it across the *palm* part of the hand. Turn your hand over as before, closing your fingers to hold the card.

(This leaves the *printed side up* inside your hand, because the card was lying on your palm instead of your fingers, and thus was not turned over when you closed your fingers while turning your hand.)

Again push the card through your closed left hand with your thumb. As the card comes out the other side of your hand, the printing suddenly appears. "There it is," you say, as you draw the card out of your hand, show it, and give it to someone. "Onset printing—it works like magic."

OTHER WAYS TO DO IT

It's All Yours

You open an envelope, take out a small card, turn the card over to show that it is blank on both sides, and slide it back into the envelope.

"Now I want you to think of a word, any word at all," you say to one of the persons watching. "Don't tell me what it is. Just fix that single word in your mind and try to form a mental picture of it."

Holding up the envelope, you explain, "I'm going to try to capture a picture of that word of yours and instantly develop it on the blank card in this envelope." You lift the envelope between your hands, as if you were holding a camera, and pretend to take a picture with it. "Let's see if I've caught an impression of it."

Opening the envelope, you remove the card, and hold it up close so the person can look at it, but for a moment you don't show it to anyone else. What the person sees now, printed on what was the blank card, is the word YOURS. "Is there now one word printed upon it?" you ask. "Please tell everybody . . . is that word *yours?*"

You wait a second for the answer, and then turn the card and hold it so the others can see the YOURS printed on it, and say, "That's certainly *yours.*"

For this make-believe mind reading stunt that turns into a magical joke, you will need a 3″ × 5″ office index file card, blank on both sides, and an envelope to hold it. Set it up ahead of time by printing YOURS in big letters on one side of the card. Turn the envelope flap-side up, slide the card into it with its printed side down, and put the envelope into a pocket or purse.

Start the trick by taking out the envelope and holding it in your left hand, face down with its flap toward the right. With your right hand, open the envelope and slide out the card, keeping it flat so as not to reveal the printing on its underside.

Hold the card in your right hand in the way previously explained, and turn your hand over to show that both sides of the card are (apparently) blank. Slide the card back into the envelope, and close the flap.

Choose someone to help you with the trick and have the person stand beside you, or select someone who is seated a little apart from the others, so you can later show the person the card without immediately letting everybody else see what is printed on it.

Ask your helper to think of any word, but not to tell you what it is, just to form a mental image of the word. "I'm going to try to capture a picture of that word of yours and instantly develop it on the blank card in this envelope," you explain, as you hold up the envelope like a camera and pretend to do that. "Let's see if I've caught an impression of it."

Turn the envelope flap-side up, remove the card, and toss aside the empty envelope. Hold the card close so the person can see the printing that has magically appeared on it, but keep its back toward the others so they can't yet see what is on it. "Is there now one word imprinted upon it?" you ask the person. "Please tell everybody . . . is that word yours?"

Wait for the answer, which leads everybody to believe for a moment that you really made the mentally chosen word appear on the card. Then slowly turn the card around, hold it for all to see the YOURS on it, and say, "That's certainly *yours.*"

This simple method can be used to make any sort of written message or small picture (such as one clipped from a newspaper or magazine and attached with rubber cement) appear on a blank card that has been placed in an envelope, to fit whatever patter-story you want to tell.

Double Dater

HOW IT LOOKS

You take out a date stamper, an ink pad, and three business cards. While your back is turned, someone sets the stamper to any month, day, and year he or she wishes, and stamps that date on the blank side of one of the cards. The person turns the card face down to hide the date that has been stamped, and then twists the wheels of the stamper to mix up all the dates.

Facing the person, you cover the card from view by sliding it between the two other cards, and you ask him or her to place a fingertip on them while thinking of the date that was stamped. You pick up the stamper, twist its wheels, and set it to a date. Then you stamp it on the card. It is the same as the hidden date the person had in mind!

THE SET-UP

Prepare one of the business cards in advance by cutting out the center of it to make a lengthwise "window" opening 1" X 2¼". Turn all three cards with their printed sides up, and sandwich the one with the cut-out center between the other two, so there is an uncut card at the top and the bottom of the packet.

Have the three cards and the ink pad in the left side pocket of your jacket, and the date stamper in the right side pocket. (If you are doing the trick in your own office, you can have the things handy in a desk drawer.)

WHAT YOU DO

Bring out the date stamper and the ink pad, put them on the table, which you are standing behind, and show how the stamper works. "You've probably seen one of these before," you say. "By pushing the little wheels around, you can set it to any of the twelve months of the year, to any of the possible thirty-one days, and to any year."

Take out the packet of business cards. Hold them, printed sides up, in your left hand. Spread the cards out a little, but be careful not to reveal the opening in the middle one.

Turn your hand over palm down, to bring the blank sides of the cards face up, and take the *bottom* card from the packet with your right hand. Place that card lengthwise, blank side up, at the center of the table. Drop the other two, stacked together, lengthwise at the back of the table, closer to you.

Explain to the person that when you turn your back, you want him or her to set the stamper to any date. "When you have chosen a date," you say, "then ink the stamper, and print that date on the card." Push the single card forward, point to the center of it, and open the lid of the ink pad.

Center cut out to make window opening

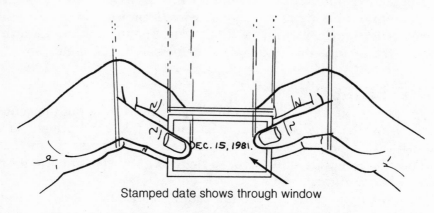

DEC. 15, 1981.

Stamped date shows through window

Squaring up the three cards by tapping bottom edges on table

Turn your back, wait for the person to print a date on the card, and say, "Please remember the date, and then turn the card over, face down on the table. . . . Now twist the wheels of the stamper to scramble all the dates. Mix them up so there is no way I can tell which date you chose."

Face the person again, put your right fingertips on the single card, and draw that across the table toward the other two cards, keeping it flat as you slide it. With your left fingers, slightly spread out the edges of the other two. Slide the single card in between them, so it is sandwiched in the middle.

With your left fingers at one side edge and right fingers at the other side edge, even up the stack of three cards. As you do that, tilt the stack upright momentarily and tap the bottom edges on the table to square them. This allows you to glance secretly at the back of the stack, where you can see the date stamped on the middle card through the "window" opening cut out of the card at the rear.

As soon as you know what the date is, immediately lay the squared-up cards flat on the table again, and say, "Will you please put the tip of your finger on these to hold the one that you stamped between them? Now think of the date you chose."

Pick up the date stamper, twist the wheels, and set it to the date you know was the chosen one. Put the stamper aside, and tell the person to remove his finger from the cards.

Place your left fingers on the left side edge of the cards to keep them squared. Slide your right fingers into the right edge, draw out the middle card, and push that to the center of the table.

Touch the stamper to the ink pad, and print the date on that face-down card. Read it aloud, and say, "This is the date that came to my mind. . . . And what was the date *you* had in mind?" Turn the card over to the other side to show the date that was originally stamped, and read it aloud to confirm that they are the same.

Hand the person the double-dated card. Pick up the others with the ink pad and stamper, and put them away in your pocket.

OTHER WAYS TO DO IT

Another View from the Window

You may prefer this way of doing the trick. In addition to the date stamper, ink pad, and *one* business card, you will need a standard "personal letter"-size envelope. At the center of the *face* of the envelope, about ½" up from the bottom edge, cut out a "window" about 1½" high and 2½" wide.

Turn the printed side of the business card up, put the card in the envelope, and stand the envelope on end in the right pocket of your jacket, with its cut-out face toward your body and flap toward the right. Have the date stamper and ink pad in another pocket.

Start the trick by taking out the stamper and ink pad, and putting those on the table. Take the envelope from your pocket, keeping its face toward you, and drop the envelope on the table with its back up and the flap toward the right. Open the flap, remove the business card, turn it blank side up, and place it lengthwise at the center of the table.

Show the person how the stamper works, and explain that when you turn your back, you want it set to any date. With your back turned, have the chosen date stamped on the card. Tell the person to turn the card face down so the date is hidden, and then ask that the wheels be twisted around to scramble all the dates on the stamper.

Face the person again, and pick up the card with your right hand, keeping it face down and close to the table. The envelope is lying where

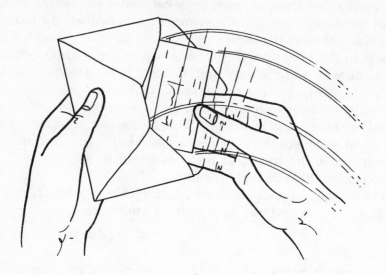

Left hand rests on table as card is put into envelope

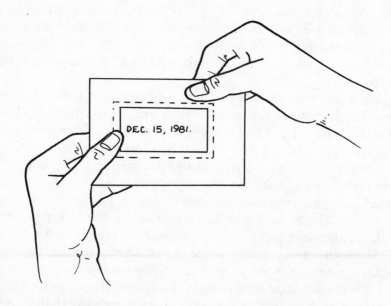

DEC. 15, 1981.

Right hand presses flap shut as left hand holds window facing you

you first placed it, its back up, and its bottom edge to the left. Put your left fingers under that edge and your thumb on top, to hold it with your knuckles resting on the table. With your right hand, slide the card into the envelope, pushing it all the way inside until it is centered over the "window." Remove your right hand.

Bring your right hand to the narrow end of the envelope that is toward you at the back of the table. Put your right thumb *under* that end, fingers on top, and draw the envelope from the left hand to lift it up with its face toward you. Take it again with the left hand, turn it horizontal, and hold it up in front of you.

With your right hand, close the flap. Run your right thumb and fingers across the top edge a couple of times as though pressing the flap shut. This gives you time to look secretly into the "window" and see the date stamped on the card inside the envelope. Just glance at the date, and immediately drop the envelope face down on the table.

Ask the person to think of the date chosen. Twist the wheels of the stamper back and forth, as though you are having difficulty "mind reading." Finally, set the stamper to the correct date, touch it to the ink pad, and lay down the stamper.

Keep the envelope flat on the table, open the flap, and remove the card, placing it on the table. Close the lid of the ink pad, put the empty envelope on top of it, and put the pad and envelope away together in your jacket pocket.

Slide the card to the center of the table, pick up the stamper, and stamp the date on the card. End the trick as before by turning the card over to show that your date exactly matches the date chosen before.

Magnetic Personality

HOW IT LOOKS

"Have you a magnetic personality?" you ask someone, as you take out three business cards and a pencil. You lay the three cards in a row on the table with their printed sides up, and place the pencil next to them. "Just for fun, let's try a little experiment in mental graphology to see if we can determine the magnetic power of your personality from your handwriting."

You explain that you will turn your back so you can't see what the person is doing. "There's nothing individual about any of those three cards," you say. "But I want you to make one of them distinctive by impressing your personality upon it."

With your back turned, you ask the person to take any one of the cards, to turn it blank side up, and to write his or her name on it with the pencil. "When you have done that, turn it face down again, and put it back where it was, so I won't know which one you wrote on," you say. "Just to confuse things a little more, switch the positions of the other two cards—the two you didn't write on. Exchange one for the other."

Then you turn around to face the person, pick up the pencil, and hold it in your fingers. You slowly move it back and forth across the row of cards, until it suddenly taps down on one of them.

"This one seems to have the strongest pull." You turn the card face up, and point to the person's name written on it. "That was the one. . . . You do have a magnetic personality."

THE SET-UP

Prepare one of the cards by making a tiny nick near the bottom of one side edge with your thumbnail. Have the nicked card and the two others in one of your pockets with a full-length pencil. The cards need not be in any special order.

WHAT YOU DO

Talk about the person's "magnetic personality" and the experiment in "mental graphology." Take out the three cards, mix them, and lay them out on the table in a well-spaced row with their printed sides up. Put the pencil beside them.

Secretly note and remember the position of the nicked card in the row, whether it is in place one, two, or three, counting across from your left to right.

Explain that you will turn your back so you can't see what is being done. Ask the person to choose any one of the three cards, to turn it blank side up, and to write his or her name on it. You want the card with the name on it put back in the same position in the row, so you say, "When you have done that, turn the card face down again, and put it back where it was so I won't know which one you wrote on."

Now you want the person to exchange the positions of the two cards that were not signed. "Just to confuse things a little more, switch the positions of the other two cards—the two you didn't write on," you say. "Exchange one for the other."

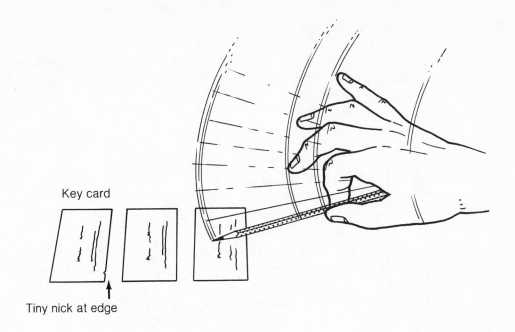

Key card

Tiny nick at edge

When the person has finished switching those two, turn around. Pick up the pencil, and hold it out horizontally by gripping the eraser end between your right thumb and first finger. Bring it down over the cards, and slowly pass it back and forth above them. That gives you plenty of time to note the final positions of the three cards in the row.

Secretly look for the nicked card. If it is still in the same position in the row as when you laid out the cards, then the nicked one is the card that the person's name is written on. But if the nicked card is *not* in its original position, then the person did *not* sign the nicked card *or* the card that is now where the nicked one was at the start. By mentally eliminating those two, you immediately know that the remaining card was the one signed.

(This is because whichever card was signed is the only one that has remained in an unchanged position in the row throughout the trick, while the positions of the other two were changed. Suppose, for example, that the nicked card was the first in the row at the start. If it is still first in the row, that is the card that was signed. But if some other card is first in the row at the finish, then the person *didn't* sign that one or the nicked one, so the signed card must be the third in the row.)

As you slowly move the pencil back and forth, pause above the card that you now know has the person's name on the other side. Relax your grip on the eraser so the pencil point suddenly tips down and taps that card. "This one seems to have the strongest pull," you say. Turn the card face up, and point to the name on it. "That was the one. . . . You do have a magnetic personality!"

OTHER WAYS TO DO IT

The Stamp Finder

"If you've ever wanted to mail a letter and couldn't find a stamp," you say, "maybe you'll be interested in the system I've worked out for finding one."

You take out a postage stamp and place it on the table, and then tear a business card into three pieces and lay those out in a row.

"But first, we have to lose the stamp. Will you lose it for me?" you ask someone. "I'll turn my back, and I want you to place the stamp under any one of those three pieces of card. Slide it in under the center of the card so it is covered and I can't tell which of the three hiding places you chose."

When the person says that has been done, you tell him or her to switch the positions of the other two pieces of card. "Just trade their places—exchange one for the other."

You then turn to face the person. "The stamp is well lost," you say. "It could be in any of those places. So now I use my system. . . . I simply ask myself where I would be if I were a stamp." You point to each of the three pieces, and then pick up one of them to reveal that the stamp is under it. "And there it is!"

There is no advance preparation for this trick. All you need is a business card and a postage stamp.

Start by placing the stamp on the table. Then turn the business card lengthwise, and fold it in thirds so you can tear it into three pieces of about equal size. That will give you a middle piece with *two* torn edges, while each of the other pieces has only one torn edge. The one with the two torn edges is your "key." It serves the same purpose as the nicked card in the previous trick.

Mix up the pieces, and lay them out on the table in a row near the stamp. Note and remember the starting position of the "key," whether it is first, second, or third in the row.

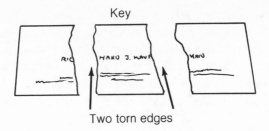

Explain to the person that when you turn your back, you want him or her to hide the stamp by sliding it under the center of any of the three pieces of card chosen. Then ask that the positions of the other two pieces be switched, traded place for place.

When that has been done, turn to face the person and secretly look for the "key." If it is still in the same position in the row as it was at the start, the stamp is under it. But if the "key" has been moved to some other position, then the stamp is *not* under the one where the "key" originally was, and it is *not* under the "key" itself. It must be under the remaining piece of card, wherever that happens to be in the row.

Point to each of the three in turn, tell the little joke about your "system" for finding the stamp, and pick up the correct piece of card to reveal the stamp that was hidden under it.

Buck Stop

"You all know the old saying that 'the buck stops here,'" you say. "If someone will please take out a dollar bill, I'll try to discover just where the buck *does* stop."

On the table, you have a stack of three paperback books, and you ask the person with the dollar to mix up the books and then lay them out in a row. You explain that when you turn your back, you want the person to slide the dollar under the bottom of any one of the books he or she chooses, to hide it beneath that book.

You turn away, and when that has been done, you ask that the positions of the other two books be switched by exchanging one for the other, and then you face the person again.

"I might guess where it is," you say. "But if I guessed, there are two out of three chances that I'd be wrong. So instead of my guessing, will you please concentrate on where you hid it, and try to direct me with your thoughts?"

You look at the person, close your eyes for a moment, and then open them and suddenly tap your finger down on one of the books. "This time, I think the buck has stopped here." You lift the book, and the dollar is under it. As you hand back the bill, you say, "Thanks for letting me read your mind."

Again, there is nothing to prepare. Just use any three paperback books or small (digest size) magazines. Stack them together on the table.

Start by asking someone to take out a dollar bill and to place it flat on the table. Then tell the person to mix up the books and to lay them out in a row. As that is being done, secretly note and remember which of the books is the first one at the left end of the row. (Since each of the books has a different cover, that book in the first position becomes your "key.")

Turn your back as the bill is slid beneath whichever book is chosen. Have the person switch the positions of the other two books by exchanging their places. Then face the person again, and glance at the final positions of the three books.

If the book that was at the left of the row is still there, you know the bill is under that one. But if that book has been moved, then the bill is *not* under whatever book is now first in the row, and it is *not* under the book that originally was first in the row. By eliminating those two, you know where it is.

Act out the rest of the trick by asking the person to "try to direct me with your thoughts," and then put your finger down on the book that has the bill hidden under it, and say, "This time, I think the buck has stopped here."

Ups and Downs

HOW IT LOOKS

You take a small stack of business cards from your pocket and invite someone to join you in a little magical game of Follow the Leader. Counting out the cards, you give five to him and keep five yourself. You fan out your five, and ask the person to make sure that his five are all facing the same way as yours, with the printing on them face up.

"Now I'll do this very slowly," you explain, "so that you can move each of your cards exactly as I do." You then move cards from the top of your packet to the bottom, turning some of them over so their blank sides are up, and keeping some with their printed sides up. You wait each time, so he can move each card just as you have.

"Since you did exactly as I did, your cards should now be the same as mine," you say. You spread your cards out to show that despite mixing them face up and face down, all five are as they were at the start, with their printed sides facing up.

But when he spreads his cards out, he finds a blank-faced card at the center of them. "You seem to have made a mistake," you tell him. "Let's try it again."

You repeat the same thing, as he closely follows each move and again turns each of his cards exactly as you do. And this time, you stop just before the final moves, so that he can check his set of cards against yours. At that point both sets match, with some face up and some face down.

But at the end, no matter how carefully he follows the identical last moves, he is tricked again. All five of yours have their printed faces up, but one of his is still turned over the wrong way, blank side up.

"It happens every time," you say, as you gather up the cards and put them back into your pocket. "Must be magic."

THE SET-UP

One of the business cards is double faced. It is easily made by fastening the blank sides of two cards together so they look like a single card. Whichever way it is turned over, there is always a printed side face up.

To make it, take two regular business cards, coat the blank side of each of them with rubber cement, and stick the two blank sides together. Make sure all the edges are exactly even and firmly cemented. Rub away any excess cement so the edges look clean.

Add the tricked card to nine more regular business cards. Turn them all with their printed sides up and stack them together so that the double card is the *ninth one down from the top* of the stack of ten.

Slide them into a card case, a section of your wallet, or just snap a rubber band around the stack and have them in one of your pockets.

WHAT YOU DO

Take out the stack of business cards and hold them in your left hand, printed sides face up. Count off the top five into your right hand, one at

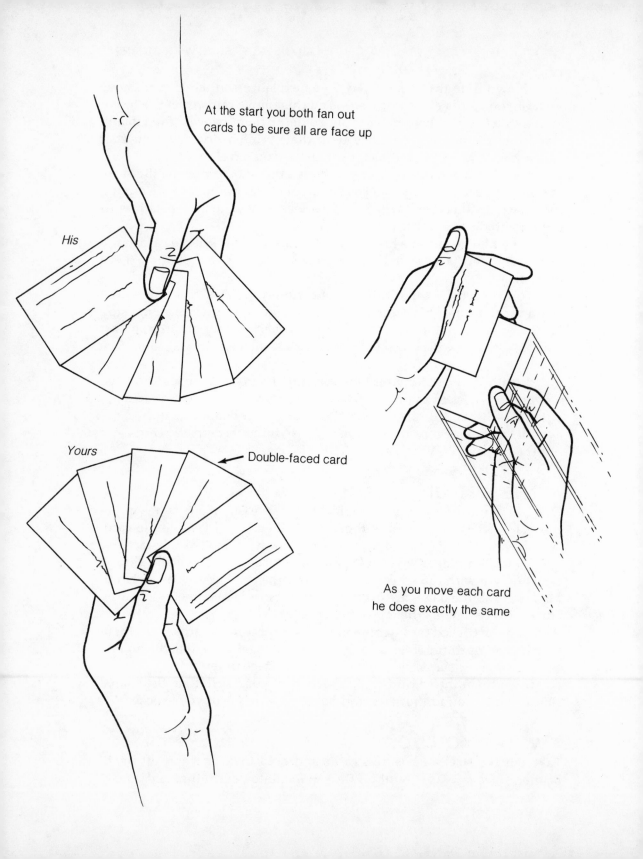

At the start you both fan out
cards to be sure all are face up

His

Yours

Double-faced card

As you move each card
he does exactly the same

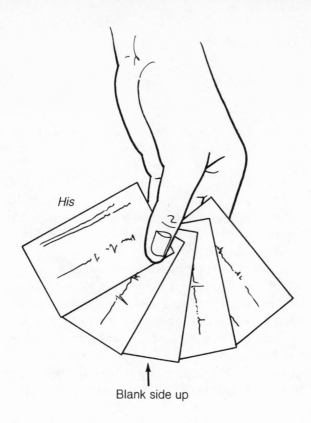

His

Blank side up

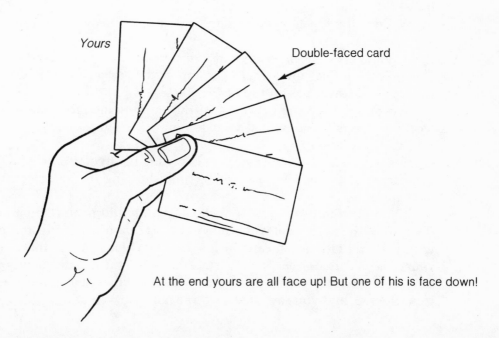

Yours

Double-faced card

At the end yours are all face up! But one of his is face down!

a time, placing them one atop another. Give those five to the other person.

Then count off the other five the same way and keep those for yourself. Counting them out that way from hand to hand automatically reverses the order of the cards, so that the double-faced card is now the *second one down from the top* of your set of five.

Hold your set flat in your left hand. With your right fingers, spread the cards open in a fan to show they are all face up, with their printed sides showing. Ask him to spread his cards out in his hand to make sure his five are all face up like yours. Close the fan, hold them flat as before, and tell him to hold his cards the same way.

Explain that he is to move each of his cards exactly as you do, one by one, and that you will make each of the moves slowly so that he can follow them as closely as possible. Pause after each step to make sure he does just what you do. Here are the moves that you make:

1. Turn over the top card of your stack, so the blank side is up, and put that at the bottom of the stack.

2. Take the next card off the top, and put that at the bottom of the stack, this time without turning it over. (Unknown to him, this card is the double-faced one.)

3. Turn over the next card, so the blank side is up, and put it at the bottom of the stack.

4. Move the next card from the top to the bottom without turning it over.

5. Turn the top card over, blank side up, and leave it on top of the stack.

6. Now turn the *entire stack* of five cards over in your hand.

7. For the final move, turn the top card over so its printed side is face up, and leave that on top of the stack.

Despite the repeated turning of the cards, some face up and some face down, when you spread your five out in a fan they all have their printed sides face up.

But when he does the same and spreads his five out, he finds that one card is face down with its blank side showing in the center of his face-up cards.

"You seem to have made a mistake," you tell him, and, to point out the mistake he has made, you remove the *top card* of your five and point with it to the face-down card in his packet. Then you put that card of yours back at the *bottom* of your stack of five. This gesture leaves your cards set up as they were at the start, with the double-faced card second from the top, and you say, "Let's try it again."

Ask him to turn his "wrong" card over so all of his are face up like yours. Repeat the moves 1 through 4, as he again follows you step by step. But this time, after you both have completed move 4, say, "Let's make sure you have followed me so far."

Spread your cards open in a fan, and ask him to do the same. At this point, his set of cards matches yours; in both sets, the second and fourth cards from the top are face down, and the others are all face up. "Good," you say. "You've matched me exactly up to now. Just watch me closely and do what I do."

Close your fan of cards, and wait for him to close his. Then go on with the final moves, 5, 6, and 7, as he does the same with his cards. Spread yours out in a fan to show that they are all with their printed faces up.

But when he fans his out, he discovers that he has gone wrong again. He still has one card face down at the center of his face-up cards.

"It happens all the time," you say, as you take both sets of cards and put them away in your pocket. "Must be magic."

OTHER WAYS TO DO IT

With Picture Post Cards or Personal Photos

Instead of business cards, you can do the same trick with any kind of small advertising cards that are printed on one side and blank on the other—or with picture post cards, or a stack of personal photos that you just "happen to have" in an envelope in your pocket.

Ahead of time, make one that is double faced by cementing two together back to back, and put that one ninth down from the top of the stack of ten. Then follow the same moves as with the business cards.

With Dollar Bills

You can use dollar bills, or play-money bills, by making a double-faced one of those. Instead of rubber cement, you may want to use double-stick transparent tape (sticky on both sides) to fasten the pair smoothly together.

The ten bills, including the double-faced one, should be kept stacked flat in your wallet, *not folded*, so they remain flat when you hold them in your hand as you do the trick. Crisp new bills are best to use.

Direct Link

HOW IT LOOKS

You take out two business cards, show each of them separately, then fold them together, and tear out their entire centers.

"Imagine that these are two miniature picture frames," you say, as you open them out and hold one in each hand. "Imagine that this one is an abstract of inner space, and that this one represents outer space."

You lay one across the other. "Now if you can imagine that, then maybe you can also imagine this—that one has become joined to the other, like the two links of a chain."

Slowly drawing them out, you show that they have become linked, and then shake them so one hangs dangling down from the other. "A space-link mobile." Quickly you tear through one of the cards, separate them, and drop them on the table. "The magic of imagination."

THE SET-UP

One of the cards is prepared in advance by your tearing it slightly, which leaves an edge slit open after the centers of the cards are torn out during the showing of the trick.

Turn a card with its printed face up, and its narrow ends at the top and bottom. At its right edge, just below the middle, make a horizontal tear about half an inch long, from that edge in toward the center. Press the torn parts together again, and flatten them with your thumb and fingers.

Place another card on top of that one, and put the two on top of a small stack of cards. You can carry them in a card case, in your wallet, or put a rubber band around them and have them in one of your pockets.

WHAT YOU DO

Remove the two top cards from the stack, spreading them slightly to slide them off together. Lay them vertically on your left palm, and put

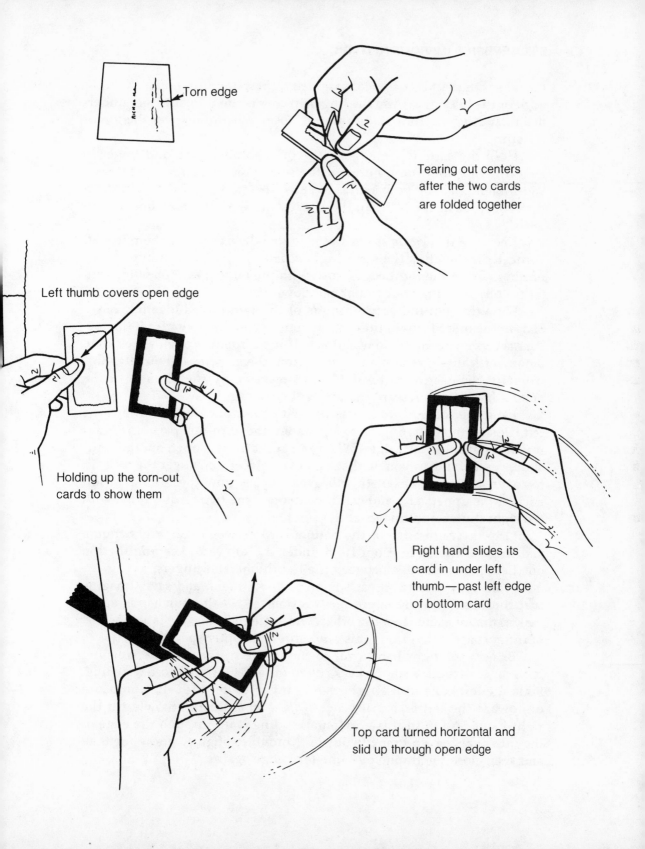

Torn edge

Tearing out centers
after the two cards
are folded together

Left thumb covers open edge

Holding up the torn-out
cards to show them

Right hand slides its
card in under left
thumb—past left edge
of bottom card

Top card turned horizontal and
slid up through open edge

the rest of the cards away. Slide your right first fingertip under the right edge of the bottom card so the fingertip covers the torn slit from underneath, and as you draw that card out, close your thumb over the top of the slit.

Hold the card at the edge with your thumb on top and fingertip beneath, and hold the other card the same way with your left thumb and finger. Separate your hands to show the cards, and then put them back together in the left hand as they were, with the torn one underneath.

Keep the two cards stacked evenly together, and fold them in half vertically by bending the right edges *down away from you* and up underneath, to bring the right edges flush with the left edges. Crease the center fold by running your thumbnail down it.

Now tear out the entire centers of the two folded-together cards. Start at the folded side, a little less than half an inch down from the top. Tear across horizontally to within a half-inch from the open edges, then down vertically to within a half-inch from the bottom, and, finally, horizontally back across to the fold. This leaves only the "frame" of the outer edges intact. Discard the torn-out centers.

Hold the folded cards vertically with their open edges toward the left. Place your left fingertips up under the torn-out part, and your thumb against the left edges. With your right thumb, open out the cards at the center, and, as you do that, slide your left thumb over the torn slit to cover it. Keep that left thumb over what is now the torn-apart left edge of the upper card, and continue to open the two cards out flat with the right thumb and fingers at the right edges.

Grip the right edge of the bottom card between your right thumb and fingers, and slide it out from under the top card, keeping the top one held at its left edge between the left thumb and fingers.

Hold up one card in each hand to show them, and say, "Imagine that these are two miniature picture frames." With your hands apart, look at first one and then the other. "Imagine that this one is an abstract of inner space . . . and that this one represents outer space."

Bring your right hand over to the inside of the left one, keeping both cards vertical, with the backs of your hands toward those watching. Slide the left edge of the right-hand card in under the left thumb and on toward the left *beyond the edge of the card beneath it.* Slowly tilt the right-hand card until it is horizontal, sliding it up through the edge of the other card as you move your left thumb enough to allow for that, and then close the thumb over the torn edge again.

"Now if you can imagine that, then maybe you can also imagine this," you say, as you lower your hands and draw the right-hand card on up to the top of the other one to show them linked. "One has become joined to the other, like the two links of a chain."

Move the cards back and forth, and then take your right hand away. With your left hand, shake the joined cards so one dangles from the other. "A space-link mobile."

Bring your right hand up to where the left thumb and fingers are holding the torn edge together. Grip that edge, and quickly pull it down as if tearing it apart. Separate the two cards, drop them singly on the table, and say, "The magic of imagination."

OTHER WAYS TO DO IT

Ring a Dangle

You borrow a finger ring, then take out a business card, fold the card in half, and tear out its center, leaving only a rectangular frame.

Placing the ring in the hand that is holding the card, you give the ring and card a shake, and the ring links through the card and hangs dangling from it. You tilt the card to slide the linked ring back and forth, and finally tear the card apart to remove the ring and return it to its owner.

Prepare a card in advance by turning it with its narrow ends top and bottom, and tearing a half-inch *diagonal* slit just below the middle of the *left* edge, from that edge in toward the center. Flatten out the tear with your thumb and fingers, and put that card on the *bottom* of a small stack of cards.

Start by borrowing a ring. Place it on the table and bring out the stack of cards. Hold them in your right hand. With your left first finger and thumb, draw out the bottom card, gripping it between the fingertip underneath and thumb on top to cover the slit left edge. Show the card, front and back, and put away the rest of the cards.

Fold the card in half vertically from right to left. Hold the card flat against the left fingers with the left thumb, and crease the center fold by running your right thumbnail down it. Tear out the entire center of the card in the way previously explained, and discard the torn-out scraps, leaving only the folded frame.

Hold the folded frame vertically between the left thumb and fingers at the left edges, and lift your hand so its back is toward those watching. With your right hand, open out the center fold, and at the same time, slide your left thumb over the torn-apart slit to cover it.

Keep your left hand as it is, with the palm toward you, holding up the opened-out frame to show it, and remove your right hand to pick up the ring from the table.

Bring your right hand over inside the left hand. Slide your left thumb upward slightly, to keep hold of the upper part of the card's left edge, and press the *back* of the nail of your left little finger against the card's bottom left edge, which tilts the lower part open at the slit.

With your right hand, put the ring through the slit and down over the lower part of the card's left edge, to leave the ring resting against the left little finger. Then use the tip of your right thumb to push the slit back together, and slide your left thumb down to cover the slit and to hold it firmly.

Remove your right hand. Hold the card and ring as they are, momentarily, with your left hand. Then give the card a sudden downward shake, and lift your left little finger to let the ring drop into view, hanging linked to the bottom edge of the card. Turn your left hand to bring the card horizontal, and tilt it back and forth as the linked ring slides around it.

Finally bring your right hand up to where the left thumb and fingers are holding the torn edge together. Grip that edge, and pull it open as if tearing it apart. Remove the ring, return it to its owner, and drop the torn-apart card on the table.

The Acrobatic Paper Clips

HOW IT LOOKS

You place four paper clips in a row on a desk or table. Picking them up one at a time, you put three into your left hand, and the fourth one into your pocket.

"How many are in my hand?" you ask. The answer is three, but you open your hand to show that all four clips are in it.

You repeat the same thing, putting three, one at a time, into your left hand, and the fourth into your pocket. Again you open your hand to show that the fourth one has returned to join the three that were there.

"This time, we'll try something different," you say, as you take all four clips from your left hand and put them one at a time into your pocket. You snap the fingers of your right hand four times, and say, "They're all back again . . . and while they were flying through the air, they joined like acrobats and linked themselves together into a chain!"

You draw the four clips out of your left hand, and hold them up to show them chain-linked to one another.

THE SET-UP

This is a trick to do in an office, or someplace where you know there is a box or dish of paper clips handy. If you do it in your own office, you can have an open container of clips on the desk or in a drawer.

All you have to do secretly ahead of time is to link four clips together into a chain, and put those into the empty right pocket of your jacket.

WHAT YOU DO

Dip your right fingers and thumb into the container of clips. While you are fingering them, secretly push one of the clips up against the inside of your fingers with your thumb, closing your two middle and little fingers loosely around the clip to hold it hidden in them. Then take out four clips, one at a time, with your first finger and thumb, and lay them down in a spaced-apart row.

Hold your left palm up, fingers toward the front. Pick up one of the four clips with your right thumb and first finger, and put it into your left hand, closing the hand as you say, "One in my hand."

Pick up a second one with your right hand, and open your cupped left hand enough so your right hand can go down into it. As you deposit the second clip, let the hidden one secretly drop from your right hand with it, so the two go together into your left hand. There are now three in the left hand, but you say, "Two in my hand." Pick up another one, put it into your left hand, again closing that hand, and say, "Three in my hand."

Now pick up the last clip from the table with your right hand, and say, "And the fourth one goes into my pocket." Show it, and put that

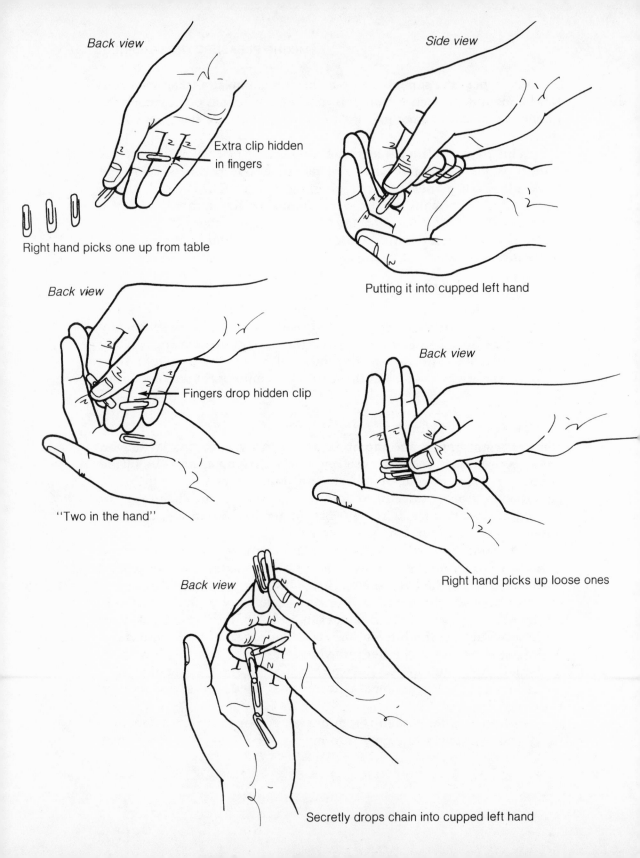

Back view

Extra clip hidden in fingers

Right hand picks one up from table

Side view

Putting it into cupped left hand

Back view

Fingers drop hidden clip

"Two in the hand"

Back view

Right hand picks up loose ones

Back view

Secretly drops chain into cupped left hand

hand into your jacket pocket as if to leave the clip there. But instead of leaving it in your pocket, just keep it hidden in your fingers, and immediately bring your hand out again and let it fall to your side for a moment.

Hold out your closed left hand, and ask, "How many are in my hand?" When the person answers, "Three," turn your hand over and count aloud as you place the clips one at a time on the table: "One, two, three . . . four." Then turn that empty hand palm up, and say, "I'll do it again."

Pick up one clip from the table with your right hand, and put it into the left. "One in my hand." Pick up another, and put that into your cupped left hand, letting the hidden clip in your right hand secretly drop with it. "Two in my hand." Pick up a third, and put that into your cupped left hand. "Three in my hand." Take the last one from the table, and say, as before, "And the fourth one goes into my pocket."

Show the clip, and put your hand into your pocket. But this time, really drop the clip into your pocket, leave it there, and scoop up the linked chain of four so they are hidden in your fingers. Immediately bring your hand out again, and let it fall to your side. Just keep your fingers loosely closed around the bunched chain, the same way you previously held a single clip.

Once more, ask, "How many are in my hand?" The person may say there are three, or perhaps four. Whatever the answer, open your left hand to show the clips lying on it. Bring your right hand over, and with the first finger spread out the clips on the left palm, pointing to each as you count the four aloud. Then say, "This time, we'll try something different."

With your right first finger, push the four clips together into a bunch on your left palm, and cup your left fingers to close that hand partly. Pick up the bunched clips between your right first finger and thumb, still inside your partly closed left hand, and as you do that, secretly drop the chain of four into the left hand. Take your right hand away, holding the bunch of loose clips between finger and thumb, and turn your closed left hand over to rest it knuckles-down on the table.

Drop the bunch of loose clips from your right hand to the table, spread them out, and say, "I'll put all four of them into my pocket." Do that, showing each clip as you pick it up from the table, and showing your right hand empty each time you take it out of your pocket to pick up another clip.

Finally hold your right hand above your closed left hand, and snap your fingers four times. Reach into your left hand, and draw out the linked chain of four. "They're all back again," you say, as you hold the chain by one end, dangling from your right hand. "And while they were flying through the air, they joined like acrobats and linked themselves together!"

OTHER WAYS TO DO IT

Setting It Up to Do Anywhere

If you want to do the trick where there may not be a box or dish of paper clips available, you can carry a small bunch of them in your pocket by having them in a sliding-drawer type pocket matchbox with a rubber band around it. That way, loose ones won't get mixed up with the linked chain of four that is also in your pocket.

At the start of the trick, just put the matchbox on the table, remove the rubber band, and slide the whole drawer out of it so you can dip into it to get an extra clip hidden in your fingers as explained.

The Tacks Collector

HOW IT LOOKS

"The other day a fellow came into the office carrying a paper cup," you say, as you show a small paper cup and then rest it upside down on the table. "When I asked him what he wanted, he said he was a tax collector. . . . I wondered when the government had started sending people out with cups to beg for taxes, but he wasn't that kind of *tax* collector. He collected *thumbtacks*—as a hobby."

You pick up the cup, shake it upside down to show it is empty, and hold it upright in one hand. "He was checking all the office bulletin boards for unusual varieties, so I asked him if he had any *invisible* thumbtacks in his collection. He said he had never heard of those."

Suddenly you reach out with your free hand, as if catching an "invisible" thumbtack from the air. You make a tossing motion toward the cup in your other hand, and the sound of a tack falling into the empty cup is heard. You tip over the cup, and a thumbtack spills out from it to the table.

Again you shake the cup upside down to show it is empty, then hold it upright, reach out with your other hand to "catch" a tack, and toss it invisibly through the air into the cup, where it is heard to land. You spill it out on the table, and continue to produce tacks that way, until there are four on the table.

"I thought he'd be glad to add them to his collection," you say. "But he claimed there was nothing *invisible* about them. . . . He didn't want them because he could *see* them!" You crumple the cup and toss it into a wastebasket. "Tacks collectors!"

THE SET-UP

You will need a small (five-ounce) paper cup and four thumbtacks, the latter preferably with heads of different colors.

Fasten the four tacks in a row about an inch below the inside top rim of the cup by pushing the point of each tack through the side of the

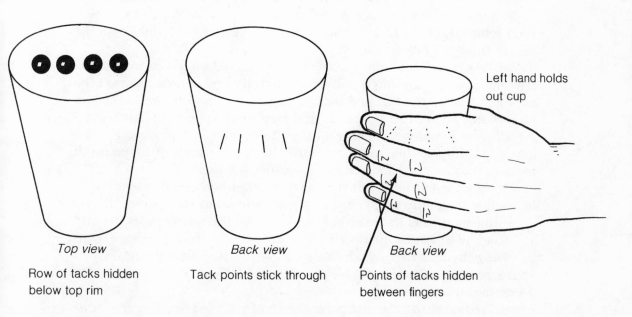

Top view

Row of tacks hidden
below top rim

Back view

Tack points stick through

Back view

Points of tacks hidden
between fingers

Left hand holds
out cup

cup. Push them through from the *inside* to the *outside*, so the heads are flat against the inside and the points extend outside. They should be closely spaced, but the heads should not overlap.

Move the tacks around in the holes until they hold securely but are also loose enough so that you can push them into the cup by applying light pressure to the points with your finger. Be careful not to prick yourself. Fixed this way, the tacks will stay in place, and the cup can be gently shaken upside down and handled quite freely.

Turn the cup mouth down, tack points to the rear, and put it on a shelf or into a drawer where you can keep it out of the way until you are ready to bring it to the desk or table you will use when you do the trick.

WHAT YOU DO

Start with the cup in your right hand, holding it upright, with the tack points toward the back. Turn the cup over, mouth down, by turning your hand over sidewise from right to left. (Turning it over sidewise conceals the inside of the cup from direct front view.) Shake the cup gently upside down, to indicate that it is empty, and then place it mouth down on the table.

As you say, "So I asked him if he had any *invisible* thumbtacks in his collection," lift the cup again with your right hand, and turn it over from left to right to bring it mouth upward. Keep it held high, with the mouth tilted slightly toward you.

Hold up your left hand, palm to the front and fingertips toward the left, and put the cup into that hand so that the row of tack points at the back go between the first and second fingers. Close your left thumb and fingers around the cup to hold it, and take away your right hand.

(The tack points are now hidden between your fingers that are around the cup so that you can handle the cup freely, turning your left hand to the front or back without revealing the points.)

Hold your left hand out to the left of your body, and keep the cup held high. Suddenly reach out into the air with your right hand, closing your fingers as though "catching" an invisible thumbtack from the air.

Keep your hands apart and make an upward tossing motion, as if throwing the tack through the air into the cup in your left hand. Open your right fingers to show it has "gone," and look up into the air as you pretend to follow its flight.

Secretly, behind the cup, press the tip of your left first finger against the point of the first tack in the row, and push the point right through so the tack falls free and is heard as it drops inside the cup. (Again, be careful not to prick your finger.) Give the cup a little shake to rattle the tack around in the bottom of it.

Now bring the cup down to the table, turning your left hand over sidewise from left to right. Touch the mouth of the cup to the table, and spill out the tack that has appeared. Hold the cup mouth down, shake it a little to indicate it is empty, and then lift it again, turning it sidewise to bring it upright. Hold the cup out to the left of your body as before.

Repeat the same thing three more times, pretending each time to "catch" a tack from the air with your right hand and to toss it invisibly into the cup in your left hand, until you have produced all four tacks, one at a time, spilling each of them out on the table.

"I thought he'd be glad to add these to his collection," you say. "But he claimed there was nothing *invisible* about them. . . . He didn't want them because he could *see* them." Crumple the cup, discard it by tossing it into a wastebasket or stuffing it into your pocket, and shake your head. "Tacks collectors!"

OTHER WAYS TO DO IT

Pushpin Penetration

You show a small paper cup and a saucer. Tipping the cup over, you spill out a bulletin board pushpin. You turn the empty cup mouth down, and stand it on the empty saucer. Then you stick the pushpin into the bottom of the inverted cup, so the pin stands upright, in full view.

You cover the pushpin with your fingers and seem to push it right through the solid bottom of the cup, and as it penetrates the cup, it is heard to fall down inside to the saucer. Stepping back, you invite someone else to lift the cup and discover the pushpin on the saucer. The bottom of the cup is undamaged, except for the tiny pinhole left at the center.

For this, you will need a small paper cup, a saucer or ashtray, and two look-alike pushpins, the kind with bright-colored plastic knobs.

Turn the cup mouth up, take one of the pushpins, and, near the inside bottom of the cup, push the pin through the side, so the knob is flush inside and the point extends outside. This holds the pushpin hidden in place the way the tacks were held in the previous trick, but inside

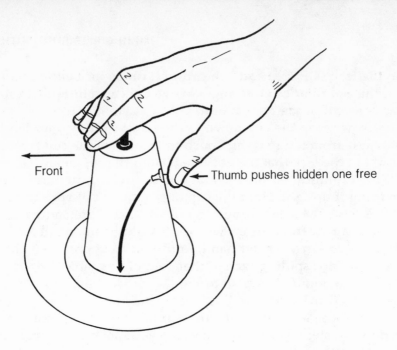

Front

Thumb pushes hidden one free

the bottom edge. Work the pushpin around in the hole as explained before, so that it is loose enough to push into the cup.

Stand the upright cup on the saucer, turn it with the pinpoint to the back, and drop the duplicate pushpin into the cup.

Start the trick by placing cup and pushpin on a table, with the pinpoint kept toward the rear. Pick up the cup with your right hand, turn it over, and spill the loose pushpin out on the saucer. Shake the inverted cup to indicate that it is empty, and stand it mouth down on the saucer.

Pick up the pushpin, show it, and push the point into the center of the cup's bottom to leave the pin standing upright there. Remove both hands for a moment so the pin can be clearly seen. Then bring your left hand down, and put your thumb and fingers around the sides of the cup to hold it steady on the saucer.

Now bring your right hand, palm down, over the bottom of the cup, so that your fingertips cover the upright pushpin and the tip of your thumb, underneath at the back, touches the point of the one hidden inside the cup. The underside of your right middle finger should lie directly over the top of the knob of the upright pushpin.

Secretly push your thumb against the point, being careful not to prick yourself, so the hidden one falls free and is heard to drop down inside the cup to the saucer. *At the same time,* grip the knob of the upright pin between the sides of your first and third fingers, with the middle finger covering the top of it. Pull the pin up out of the cup's bottom as you draw your hand back away from the cup, so the pin is hidden in your fingers. Take away your left hand, and let both hands fall to your sides as you step back from the table.

Ask someone to lift the cup to reveal the duplicate pushpin lying on the saucer. Don't be in a hurry to get rid of the other one that is hidden in your fingers.Wait until attention is on the things on the table, then casually put both hands into your jacket pockets, rest them there for a moment, and leave it behind in your right pocket as you bring your hands out again.

CHAPTER 5

WITH BORROWED MONEY

Staple Chase

HOW IT LOOKS

"I'd like to borrow a quarter—two bits," you say to someone. "But before I take it, will you please look at the date on your quarter and remember it?" Taking the coin, you wrap it in a facial tissue, snap a rubber band around the tissue, and put that on the table.

Then you bring out a small stapler and two index file cards. You show each of the cards on both sides, staple them together around all their edges, and stand them on end in your outer breast pocket, where they remain in view. (If you aren't wearing a jacket with a breast pocket, just leave the stapled cards in view on the table.)

"I'll now pay you back the two bits I borrowed," you tell the person. Picking up the tissue-wrapped quarter, you remove the rubber band and tear two small pieces from the tissue. "There you are. . . . One bit . . . two bits." You offer the person the two little torn pieces, and then quickly rip the rest of the tissue into shreds and scatter the empty scraps. "Four bits . . . six bits . . . eight bits. Bit by bit, your quarter has disappeared!"

You hand the person the stapled-together file cards, and ask him or her to tear them open. When that is done, the vanished quarter is found inside them. "Please check the date," you say, "to make sure *those* two bits are yours."

THE SET-UP

You will need a facial tissue, a rubber band, two 3" × 5" file cards, and a small stapler. Stack the two cards together and put them lengthwise into the left side pocket of your jacket. Put the rubber band and tissue into the same pocket, and put the stapler into your right side pocket (or have it handy on the table).

WHAT YOU DO

Borrow a quarter, and ask the lender to look at the date and remember it. Take out the tissue and open it out. Hold your left hand palm upward in front of you. Drape the tissue over your palm, and lay the quarter on it. Grip the quarter through the tissue from underneath, between the tip of your left thumb at the back and the tips of your fingers in front, and hold the coin upright by its bottom edge. Show it that way so everybody can see it at the center of the tissue.

The bottom edge of the coin now rests in a little fold of tissue between your thumb and fingertips. Bring your right hand to the top edge of the upright coin, and push it down as though pushing it into that fold. But really push it right down *through* the tissue, so that the coin falls into your left hand, which is still covered by the tissue. This takes hardly any pressure, because the bottom edge of the pushed-down coin easily tears through the bottom of the tissue fold that is gripped between your thumb and fingers.

With both hands still together, fold up the tissue with your right hand as though the coin were inside it, bunching it into a wad with the torn part at the center. Close your left fingers around the coin to hide it,

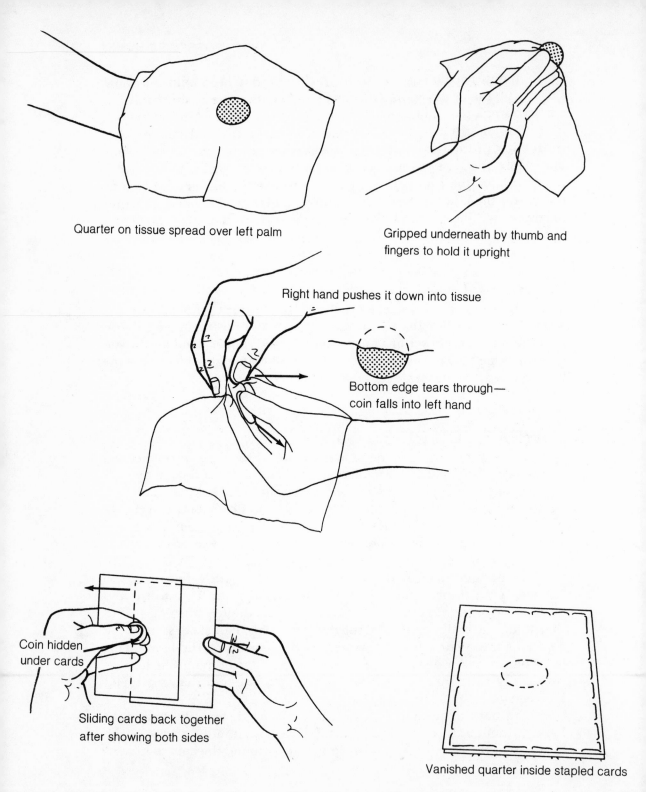

Quarter on tissue spread over left palm

Gripped underneath by thumb and fingers to hold it upright

Right hand pushes it down into tissue

Bottom edge tears through— coin falls into left hand

Coin hidden under cards

Sliding cards back together after showing both sides

Vanished quarter inside stapled cards

and take the wadded tissue with your right hand to hold it up and show it, as you let your left hand fall to your side with the concealed coin.

Say, "I'll put a rubber band around it." Put your left hand into your pocket, leave the coin in the pocket, and bring out the rubber band. Wrap the band around the tissue, and place it to one side of the table.

Take out the stapler and put that on the table. With your left hand, reach into your left pocket and slide the quarter up against the back of the index cards. Hold the quarter flat, under your fingers that are pressed to the back of the cards and with your thumb down over the face of them, and take out the cards. Turn your hand palm upward, and bring it down in front of you to show the cards.

The quarter now lies hidden beneath the cards on your left fingers, with the left thumb across the face of them. With your right hand, slide off the top card. Turn it over, and hold it up to show both sides. Then slide that card back under the other card on the left hand, *between* it and the hidden coin. Slide the next card off the top, show both sides, and slide it back under the other card in your left hand, but slide it in *beneath* the hidden coin, so the quarter is between the two cards.

Press your left thumb on the top card to hold the quarter in place between the two cards. Pick up the stapler with your right hand, and quickly staple the two cards together around all their edges. Start by fastening staples along the right and bottom edges as you hold the cards flat. You can then turn the left edge to the top and hold the cards upright, and the hidden coin won't slide out as you finish the stapling.

Put the stapler aside. Hold up the stapled-together cards. Show them and place them on the table, or turn them on end and put them partway down into your outer breast pocket, so they stick up out of the pocket and remain in view.

Pick up the wadded tissue from the table. Remove the rubber band, toss it aside, and say, "I'll now pay you back the two bits I borrowed." Tear two small pieces from the tissue. "There you are.... One bit ... two bits." Hold the pieces out as if offering them to the person, but then drop them and quickly continue ripping the tissue into shreds, pulling it apart in small bunches between your hands. "Four bits ... six bits ... eight bits." Toss the scraps away, letting them scatter, and brush your empty hands together. "Bit by bit, your quarter has disappeared!"

Take the stapled cards from your breast pocket. Give them to the person and tell him or her to tear them apart. When the vanished quarter is found inside, ask the person to please check the date on it "to make sure *those* two bits are yours."

Stapled Borrowed Bill

You can do the trick with a borrowed dollar bill instead of a quarter, if the bill is folded so it can be handled the same way as the coin. Have the things set up in your pockets as before, and start by asking to borrow a dollar.

"Please look at the serial number on your bill—not the whole thing, just the last three digits of that number," you say. "Will you read them aloud—and will somebody please remember those three numbers?"

While the person is doing that, take the facial tissue from your pocket, shake it out, and put it on the table for a moment. Repeat aloud the three numbers that are read, and take the bill. Hold it lengthwise, and fold it in half from top to bottom, then in half from left to right, and twice more in half from left to right. Crease the folds flat with your thumbnail.

Drape the tissue over your left palm, place the folded bill on the tissue, and grip it from underneath between your left thumb and fingers to hold it upright in the center of the tissue. Push it down into the tissue with your right fingers, secretly pushing it through into your left hand, and continue with the rest of the trick as though the folded bill were the quarter.

Leave the bill in your pocket as you reach into it for the rubber band, wind the band around the tissue, and place that to one side of the table. Handle the index cards as with the coin, stapling them together with the hidden bill between them, and putting them on end in your outer breast pocket or placing them in view on the table.

Rip the tissue into shreds to show that the dollar has vanished, and hand the person the stapled-together cards to tear open and discover the missing bill. Ask that the last three digits of the serial number be read aloud to confirm that it is his or her dollar.

The Ghost of Money Departed

HOW IT LOOKS

You show two paper coffee cups, and, with your hands obviously empty of anything else, you hold up a cup in each hand so those watching can look inside the cups and see that they also are empty. Stacking the cups together, you place them on the table, and say, "Let's hold a séance— and try to raise a ghost."

You ask your viewers to be very quiet and to listen for the slightest whisper. Picking up the cups again, you hold them mouth to mouth, slowly tilting them back and forth. A "whispering" sound of something sliding inside the cups is heard.

"Have you ever been haunted by the thought of all the money you spend and never see again?" you ask, as you tilt the cups up and down more rapidly, and a louder sound is heard. "What you're hearing is the ghost of money departed."

You take the cups apart, reach into one of them, and pull out a dollar bill. "There's our ghost," you say, as you show the bill and then fold it and put it away in your pocket. "I hope he's still visible when I try to spend him."

THE SET-UP

You will need two ordinary "hot drink" paper cups, the kind used for coffee. These have bottoms that are about one-quarter inch above the lower rims. The dollar bill, folded so it won't pop open, rests hidden in that recessed rim space behind the bottom of one of the cups as you hold them up with their mouths to the front to show their insides are empty.

Turn a dollar bill lengthwise, fold it in half from left to right, and in half again the same way. Fold the top third down vertically from top to center, and the bottom third up from bottom to center. Tuck the top fold inside the bottom fold, and crease all the folds tight by running your thumbnail along them so the bill stays flat and compact.

Carry the folded bill in one of your pockets and, at some time before you do the trick, secretly place it flat inside the bottom of one of the cups. Drop the other cup down into the one with the bill in it and then turn the stacked cups over *mouth down.* Turning them over together automatically drops the bill into its hiding place within the bottom rim of the inside cup. Leave the cups stacked mouth down on the table until you are ready to start the trick.

WHAT YOU DO

Let it be seen, without saying so, that both hands are empty. Pick up the stacked cups with your right hand around them, fingers at front and thumb at back. Hold the upper rim of the inner cup with your left thumb and first two fingers around it. Tilt the bottom of the cups back toward you at an angle, and slowly separate them by lifting off the outer

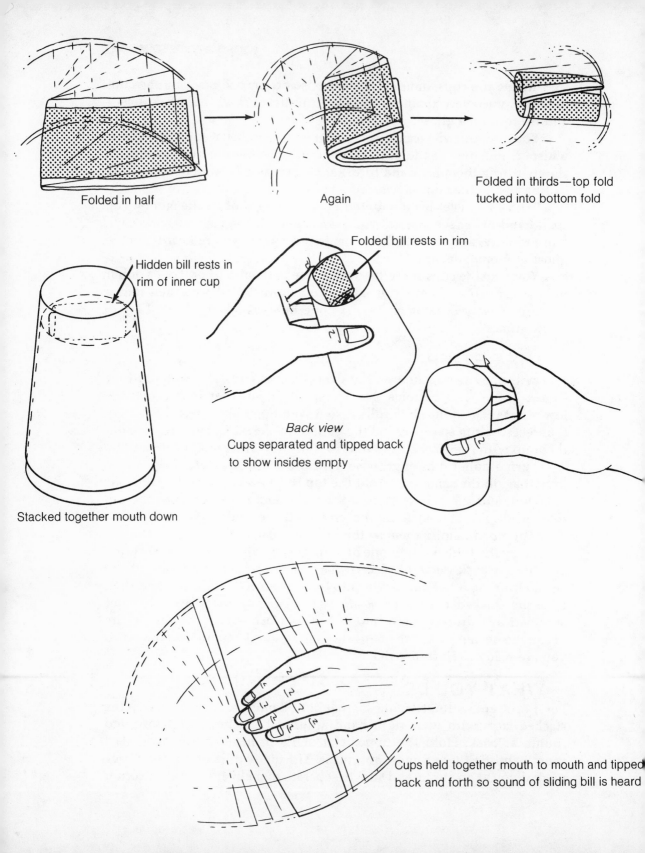

Folded in half

Again

Folded in thirds—top fold tucked into bottom fold

Folded bill rests in rim

Hidden bill rests in rim of inner cup

Back view
Cups separated and tipped back to show insides empty

Stacked together mouth down

Cups held together mouth to mouth and tipped back and forth so sound of sliding bill is heard cup with your right hand. (The folded bill now lies in the outside bottom rim of the left-hand cup, hidden from front view by the inside bottom of the cup.)

Holding a cup in each hand, move your hands apart and raise them, so those watching can look into the mouths of the cups and see that the insides are empty. Keep the cups held that way for a moment, with the cups tilted until their mouths are almost horizontally toward the front. Then put the right-hand cup over the bottom of the left-hand cup to stack them together again. Place the stacked cups *mouth up* on the table.

"Let's hold a séance," you say, "and try to raise a ghost." Lift out the top cup with your right hand. Turn it over, and place the mouth of it against the mouth of the other cup. Hold the two together mouth to mouth by putting your left hand around them. Ask everyone please to be very quiet, and to listen for the slightest whisper.

Very slowly, tilt the held-together cups back and forth, left and right, so the "whispering" sound of the bill sliding in them can be heard. "Have you ever been haunted by the thought of all the money you spend and never see again?" you ask. Shake the cups rapidly up and down, so the bill bouncing around inside makes a louder sound. "What you're hearing is the ghost of money departed."

Finally, lift off the top cup, turn it over, and slide it up over the bottom of the other one. Hold the nested cups with the left hand. Show your right hand is empty, and reach down into the inner cup. Partly open the folded bill and slowly draw it out, hooking your left first finger down inside the top of the cup to help unfold the bill as you pull it into view.

"There's our ghost!" Put down the cups, and hold out the bill between your hands. Fold the bill in half, put it away in your pocket, and say, "I hope he's still visible when I try to spend him."

OTHER WAYS TO DO IT

The Ghost Buys Coffee

This starts the same way, by your holding up the cups to show them empty, and saying, "Let's hold a séance—and try to raise a ghost."

As before, you place the cups mouth to mouth, and tilt them back and forth so a sound is heard inside them. But at the end, instead of producing a dollar bill, you look down into the left-hand cup, and say, "Our ghost seems to have left us a spirit message."

You tilt the cup over and spill out a folded slip of paper, and when you open up the paper, you discover a half-dollar inside it. Then you show the "message" written on the paper and read it aloud. It says: "Let's have a cup of coffee. I'll buy this one—John Q. Ghost."

Use a slip of paper about the size of a dollar bill. Write the "message" on the paper, turn it lengthwise, and lay the half-dollar on it, a little to the right of center. Fold the paper just as the bill was folded, crease the folds, hide it in the stacked cups, and handle the cups as you did to produce the bill.

Houdini Wasn't Here

You talk about the fact that ever since Houdini died in 1926, various groups interested in psychic phenomena have held séances to try to contact the spirit of the famed magician. With mock seriousness, you suggest holding a little séance, then show the cups are empty, place them mouth to mouth, and tilt them back and forth so a sound is heard inside them.

"Do you suppose Houdini is trying to give us evidence of his presence?" you ask. "Perhaps he'll bring us a spirit message." You tip one of the cups over, and spill out a folded slip of paper. Opening it, you show a "message" written on it, and read it aloud: "Don't be silly! Do you think I'd haunt a coffee cup?—HOUDINI."

Just write the message ahead of time on a slip of paper, fold it as the bill was folded, hide it in the stacked cups, and produce it as previously explained.

High Interest Loan

HOW IT LOOKS

"If you'll lend me one dollar for one minute," you tell someone, "I'll pay you back twenty-five percent interest for your money."

You borrow the dollar bill, crumple it into a small ball, and place it on the table. Picking it up, you hold it with your fingertips, ask the person to drape a handkerchief over the money, and then to hold the bill through the cloth.

"I promised to pay you back twenty-five percent," you say, as you reach into your pocket, bring out a quarter, and drop the coin on the table. "There it is. . . . But I didn't promise that in a risky deal like this your money might not turn into a worthless scrap of paper. Maybe you'd better take a look at your investment."

When he looks at the dollar bill he has been holding in the handkerchief, he discovers that it has turned into a ball of scrap paper.

"Instead of the quarter, would you rather have your dollar back?" you ask. "If you're wondering where it went—it's right up here." You show your hand is empty, reach into your left jacket pocket, and produce the crumpled-up dollar bill. As you pick up your quarter and hand back the dollar, you say, "Watch it carefully. Don't let it disappear again."

THE SET-UP

Ahead of time, crumple a dollar bill into a small ball, and put it into your left jacket pocket. Tear a piece about four inches square from an old newspaper or magazine, and crumple that into a ball. Drop a quarter into your empty right-hand pants or skirt pocket, and put an opened handkerchief and the paper ball into the same pocket, with the paper ball on top.

WHAT YOU DO

Borrow a dollar bill, crumple it into a small ball, and rest it on the table. Say, "We'll use my handkerchief," and reach into your pocket with your right hand. Close your little finger and the two fingers above it around the paper ball to hide it in them. Grip the handkerchief between your thumb and first finger, pull it from your pocket, and hand it to the person.

Pick up the crumpled dollar bill from the table between your right thumb and first finger, and hold it up. Ask him to shake out the handkerchief and to drape it over your hand.

As he covers your hand with the handkerchief, secretly switch the dollar for the hidden ball of paper, by pulling the dollar down into your hand with your thumb and then pushing the paper ball up in place of it. This is easy, because your hand is out of sight under the handkerchief. Close your lower three fingers around the dollar to keep it hidden in them, as the paper ball was hidden before.

Tell him to hold the "bill" through the cloth. He grips what feels like the dollar, but is really the paper ball. When he has taken hold of the handkerchief that way, remove your hand, and say, "I promised to pay you back twenty-five percent."

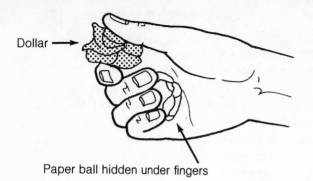

Dollar →

Paper ball hidden under fingers

Paper ball pushed up

Dollar pulled down

Switched under handkerchief

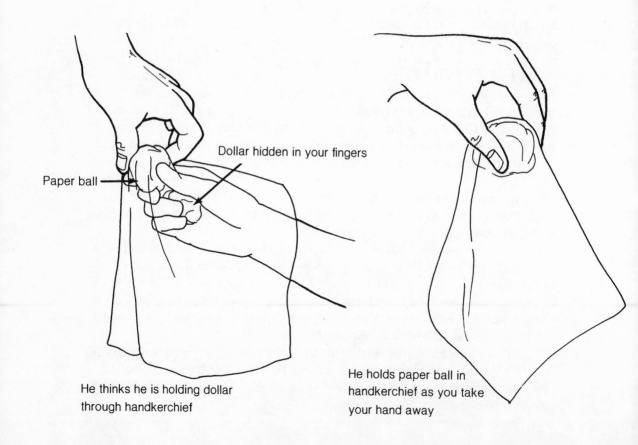

Paper ball →

Dollar hidden in your fingers

He thinks he is holding dollar through handkerchief

He holds paper ball in handkerchief as you take your hand away

Reach into your pocket, leave the hidden dollar bill in it, and bring out the quarter. Show the coin, drop it to the table, and say, "There it is."

Have him look in the handkerchief he has been holding to discover that his dollar has turned into a "worthless scrap of paper." Open out the paper ball, and give him a moment to realize his money is gone.

Ask him if he'd rather have his dollar back instead of the quarter. Then show your left hand is empty, and produce the duplicate rolled-up dollar bill from your left jacket pocket, as you say, "If you wonder where your dollar went—it's right up here." Pick up your quarter, give him the dollar, and say, "Watch it carefully. Don't let it disappear again."

OTHER WAYS TO DO IT

Handkerchief Switch Tricks

The same one-hand switch under cover of a handkerchief can be used to change a grape taken from a fruit bowl into an olive, or a red poker chip into a white one, or to "mint" money by changing a round mint candy into a nickel.

You might tear a blank sheet from a paper pad, roll it into a ball, and switch it under the handkerchief for one on which somebody's name or a written message would magically appear.

Any two small things can be switched under the handkerchief, as long as they "feel" about the same when the person holds one of them through the cloth.

Salt to Catch an Eagle

HOW IT LOOKS

"I'd like to borrow an eagle," you say. "But if nobody has an eagle, I'll settle for a quarter with a picture of an eagle on it. Has someone a quarter I can borrow?"

As you take the coin, you glance at the date and mention it, then carefully wrap the quarter in a small piece of paper so it is completely enclosed. The shape of the quarter can be seen through the paper, and the sound of it can be heard when you tap it on the table.

"There's an old saying that the way to catch a bird is to sprinkle salt on its tail," you say. "I've always wanted to try it with an eagle—do you mind if we use yours?" Taking a salt shaker from your pocket, you shake some salt on the folded paper, and put the shaker aside. "If that old saying is true, the eagle will never fly away . . . or *did* it?" You tap the paper on the table again, and there is no sound. "Maybe I didn't use enough salt. It seems to have flown."

You quickly tear up the paper and drop the empty scraps on the table. The quarter has disappeared. "Sorry. That one got away. . . . But it didn't get far."

You pick up the salt shaker, unscrew the cap, and find the missing quarter inside it. As you hand the coin back to its owner, you call attention to the date on it, and say, "Thanks for letting me borrow your eagle."

THE SET-UP

Most household salt shakers have caps large enough to hold a quarter. Remember the date on a quarter, put it into the cap of a shaker, and screw on the cap.

Cut a four-inch square of paper from an old newspaper, magazine page, or brown paper bag. Fold the bottom edge of it up until it is about three-quarters of an inch below the top edge, and crease the fold. Have the paper and salt shaker in the right-hand pocket of your jacket.

WHAT YOU DO

As you ask to borrow the quarter, take the square of paper from your pocket. Open out the bottom fold, and hold the paper on your left hand. With your right hand, take the quarter from the person. Put it on the center of the paper, and keep it in place there with the tip of your left thumb.

Glance down at the quarter as if looking at the date, and say, "1977. . . . That was a good year—for eagles." Immediately close the bottom fold up over the coin, so it is inside the square of paper at the center. (You simply ignore the date on the borrowed quarter, and mention the date of your own quarter that is in the salt shaker. Just say it casually, as a passing remark, and continue folding the paper around the coin.)

Do that by holding the paper upright, keeping the coin inside the center of the bottom fold that covers it at the back. Fold the right side of the paper out away from you, around to the front, and crease that fold. Then fold the left side of the paper around to the front, so the two ends overlap, and crease that. When making these folds, allow a little space at each side of the coin, so it will later slide freely. Finally, fold the top three-quarters of an inch of the paper down to the front, and crease that.

As you finish the folds, press your thumbs around the edges of the coin to impress the outline of it on the paper. Although the quarter appears to be completely enclosed, the folding has left an opening across the top edge at the back, so that when you later tip the paper upside down, the coin will secretly slide right out into your fingers.

Turn your right hand palm down, take the paper at that top edge between your thumb at the back and fingers in front, and drop your left hand. Bring your right hand down to the table, and tap the paper sharply several times, so the sound of the coin inside it can be heard. Press your right thumb on the coin through the paper to keep it from sliding out, and turn your right hand over, palm upward, as you lift that hand from the table to hold the paper upright.

"There's an old saying that the way to catch a bird is to sprinkle salt on its tail," you say. "I've always wanted to try it with an eagle—do you mind if we use yours?"

Bring your left hand over to take the paper, and as your hands come together, release the pressure of your right thumb, and let the quarter secretly slide out into your right hand. Lift the paper away to hold it up with your left hand, and reach into your pocket with the right hand. Leave the coin behind in your pocket, and bring out the salt shaker.

Because you pressed the shape of the coin into the paper while folding it, the outlined shape still shows, as if the quarter were still inside it. Sprinkle a little salt over the paper, and put the shaker aside on the table.

"If that old saying is true, the eagle will never fly away," you say. Tap the paper on the table again, and when no sound is heard, stare down at it. "Or *did* it?" Bend the paper back and forth a little. "Maybe I didn't use enough salt. It seems to have flown."

Take the paper with both hands, quickly tear it to bits, and drop the empty scraps on the table, as you say, "Sorry. That one got away." Pause a moment, and then add, "But it didn't get far." As you pick up the salt shaker, let it be seen that both hands are empty. Unscrew the cap of the salt shaker, take out the missing quarter, and hold it up to show it.

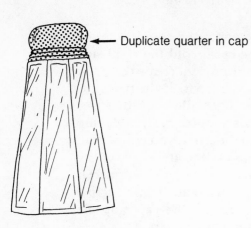

Duplicate quarter in cap

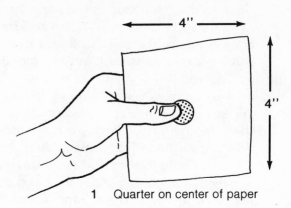

1 Quarter on center of paper

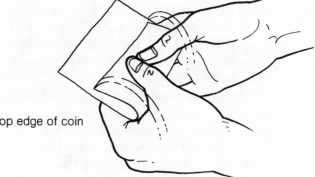

2 Bottom folded up above top edge of coin

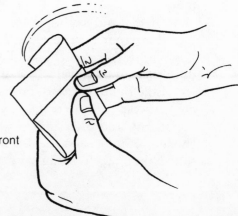

3 Right side folded around to front

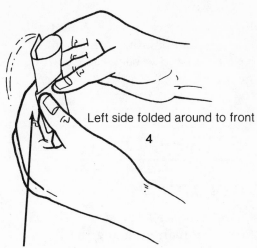

Left side folded around to front

4

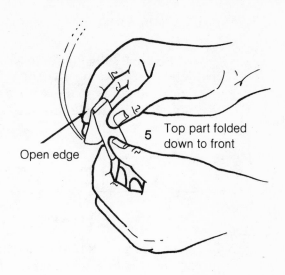

Open edge

5 Top part folded
down to front

Space between fold and edge of coin

Coin slides out into right-hand fingers

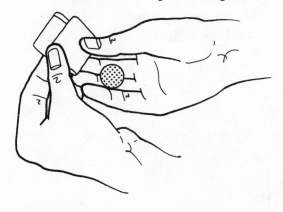

Pressed shape of coin still
seen on now-empty paper

Front view

As you hand the quarter back to the person, casually ask, "What was the date—1977, wasn't it?" (or whatever the date is). But don't look at the date yourself or make it seem important. Just give back the quarter, and say, "Thanks for letting me borrow your eagle."

OTHER WAYS TO DO IT

Pin-etration Vanish

Just have a large safety pin and the square of paper in your right-hand pocket for this one, and make sure there is a quarter among the loose change you have in some other pocket.

Start by borrowing a quarter, and as you take it, ask, "Is this a good one?" Turn it over on your hand to look at it. "There are so many counterfeits around, it's hard to tell the real ones from the fakes."

Bring out the paper, and fold the coin in it as explained previously, pressing the shape of it into the paper as you complete the folding. Tap it on the table, and say, "It sounds solid enough." Turn your right hand over to tilt the paper upside down as you hold it upright again. "But I'll be glad to test it for you."

Bring your left hand over to take the paper, and as the hands come together, let the quarter secretly slide out into your right fingers. "I have a testing instrument right here."

Reach into your pocket, drop the coin inside, and bring out the safety pin. "A very sophisticated scientific instrument." Open the pin, and turn your left hand so the outlined shape of the quarter that was pressed into the paper can be clearly seen by those watching.

Front view (hands omitted)

Holding the paper with the left hand and the pin with the right hand, push the point of the pin through the center of the paper from the back. Push it as far as it will go, and slide the penetrating point back and forth a few times.

"I was afraid of that," you say. "A real quarter wouldn't be made of metal that soft." Pull out the pin, and drop it on the table. "Any second now, it's likely to melt away and just disappear." Quickly tear the paper into bits, and drop the empty scraps. "Sorry. You seem to have lost a quarter. . . . But I won't charge you anything extra for testing it."

Wait a second. Then reach into the other pocket, bring out the handful of change, and pick out a quarter. "This one *won't* disappear," you say, as you give it to the person. "Not unless you spend it."

I've Got Your Number

HOW IT LOOKS

You take a blank card and a pen from your pocket, and put them on the table. Then you ask someone to take out a dollar bill, to wad it into a small ball, and to place that on the table. Without touching the bill, you spread a handkerchief over it so it is covered from view.

"There are some numbers that are beginning to come into my mind," you say, as you pick up the card and pen. "I get the impression of a six . . . of a three . . . of a nine. . . ." As you mention each number, you write it on the card, until you have written down a string of numbers.

You lift the handkerchief, and ask the person who lent you the bill to pick it up from the table, open it out, and look at the serial number.

Handing the card to someone else, you ask to have the numbers you wrote read aloud while the person with the bill checks them. Your "mental impressions" exactly match the serial numbers on the dollar.

THE SET-UP

Most tricks of this kind require memorizing the serial number of a duplicate dollar. This one avoids the need for that, and also eliminates handling the borrowed bill. You obviously never look at it, never touch it, and the shape of it can be seen beneath the spread-out handkerchief on the table throughout the trick.

Ahead of time, take a dollar bill of your own, and, with a pencil, print its serial number *very lightly*, but in large numerals, across the face of a business card or index file card.

Open out a handkerchief, and put it into one of your right-hand pockets. Crumple the bill, wad it into a tight small ball, and put that into the same pocket with the handkerchief. Have the card and a pen (or black crayon) in a left-hand pocket.

WHAT YOU DO

Take out the pen and card, keeping the card face down, and put them on the table. Ask someone please to take out a dollar bill. Tell the person to wad the bill into a tight little ball, and to place it on the center of the table. "I don't want to touch it myself," you say.

While he or she is doing that, reach into your pocket with your right hand. Get the duplicate rolled bill hidden at the base of your third and fourth fingers by partly closing those fingers around it. With your thumb and other fingers, take a corner of the handkerchief and pull it from your pocket. Shake it out, and pick up an opposite corner with your left hand to hold the handkerchief spread open between your two hands.

Gently lay the handkerchief flat over the wadded dollar bill that was placed on the table, spreading it out so the center of the handkerchief lies over the bill. Leave it there, and immediately pick up the pen with your right hand and the card with your left hand. Keep the penciled numbers toward you, and hold the card against the palm of the left hand.

"There are some numbers that are beginning to come into my mind," you say. "I get the impression of a six . . . of a three . . . of a nine [or whatever the penciled serial numbers happen to be]. Don't rattle off the whole sequence. Pause between calling out the numbers, as if you were having difficulty getting your "mental impressions."

This is partly to build the effect, but also to give you time to write each number carefully on the card. As you call aloud each number, trace *heavily* with the pen right over the same penciled number on the card, so the ink covers the pencil marks.

When you have finished calling out and writing all the numbers, put the pen down on the table, and, without pausing, reach for the handkerchief with the palm-down right hand. Grip the borrowed bill through the top of the cloth, lift the handkerchief by its center, and let your own hidden bill drop from your fingers at the same time. Your bill

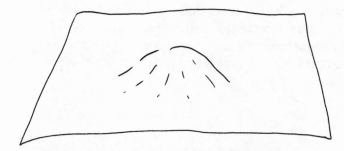

73 6 64 2 03

Lightly penciled numbers heavily
traced over with pen

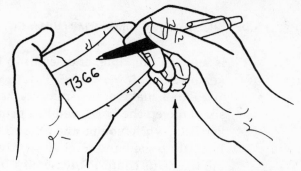

7366

Duplicate bill hidden in fingers

Borrowed bill under center of handkerchief spread flat on table

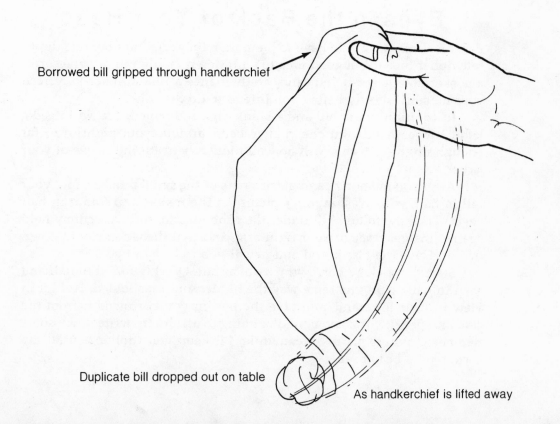

Borrowed bill gripped through handkerchief

Duplicate bill dropped out on table

As handkerchief is lifted away

is seen on the table, and seems to be the one that was under the handkerchief.

Don't make a sweeping gesture to accomplish this. All you do is simply keep the borrowed bill gripped through the center of the handkerchief, while you let the other one fall out of your fingers to the table. Just lift up the handkerchief gently, and take it away with the borrowed bill inside its center. "Please pick up the dollar and open it out," you say to the lender. "Look at its serial number."

With your left hand, give someone else the card you have been holding in that hand. Ask him or her to read aloud slowly the numbers you have written, while the person with the dollar checks them against its serial number. As the numbers are being checked, put the handkerchief back into your right-hand pocket, and leave it there with the borrowed bill still in it.

OTHER WAYS TO DO IT

Eyes in the Back of Your Head

For this version, you do have to memorize the serial number of a duplicate dollar bill. It is a good idea to jot it down on a scrap of paper or in a pocket notebook, so you can secretly glance at the number to refresh your memory shortly before you intend to do the trick.

In addition to the bill and a blank card and pencil, you will need a wide rubber band. Put the rubber band around your right arm, far enough up the arm so it will be well hidden beneath the sleeve of your jacket.

After you memorize and make a note of the serial number, fold your bill in half, with Washington's picture to the inside, and fold it in half again. Tuck the folded bill under the rubber band, so it is securely held against the *inner side* of your right arm, and pull the jacket sleeve down over it. Have the blank card and pencil in a right-hand pocket.

Start the trick by borrowing a dollar bill. Quickly fold it in half and then in half again, the same way the hidden one was folded. Hold it in view in your left hand, and give the person you borrowed it from the card and pencil. "In a moment, I'm going to ask you to write down some numbers," you explain. "Meanwhile, I'll keep your dollar behind my back, where I can't see it."

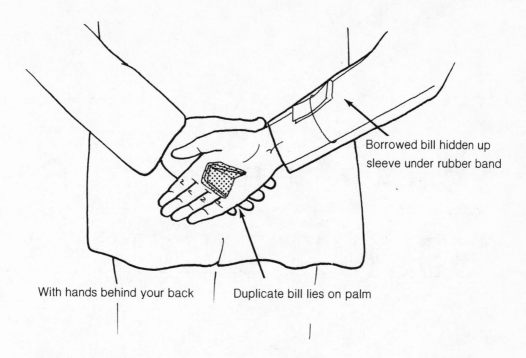

Borrowed bill hidden up
sleeve under rubber band

With hands behind your back   Duplicate bill lies on palm

Put both hands behind your back, and, after a moment, call out the first of the memorized serial numbers of the duplicate bill, saying, for example, "Will you please write down a six . . . then a five . . . and seven. . . . Those are the first numbers that come to my mind."

While you are slowly calling out the first few numbers, bring your hands together behind your back. Hold the borrowed bill in the palm of your left hand with your thumb across it. With the fingers of that hand, reach up into your right sleeve, pull the hidden bill from the rubber band, and slide it down into your right hand. Then reach into the sleeve with the left hand again, and slide the borrowed bill under the band. Rest the back of your right hand on the palm of the left hand, and keep the two loosely held together.

With your hands resting together behind your back, you can now turn around and stand with your back toward those watching, so they can see the bill lying in the palm of your right hand as you slowly call out the rest of the numbers.

Finally give the duplicate dollar to the person you borrowed the bill from, ask him or her to unfold it and check the serial numbers against the numbers written on the card to confirm that they are the same.

"Some people might think I have psychic vision," you say. "But what I really have—is eyes in the back of my head."

CHAPTER 6

SECRET DEVICES

The Pen-Clip Holder

The clip part of a pen, made for fastening the pen into a pocket, is an excellent device for holding cards, a coin, a folded dollar bill, or other things hidden in various places under your jacket so you can secretly get them into your hand. It can also be used to help switch one thing for another.

Unlike some such devices, the pen-clip holder doesn't have to be safety-pinned into place, and doesn't require removing your jacket to fix it into position. You can move around freely with little chance that whatever is clipped to it will shake loose. It holds things securely.

Here are some of the ways it can be used:

In a Back Pocket

Fasten the clip over the top edge of your right rear pants pocket, at the *outside corner* of the pocket, with the pen down inside the pocket and the clip part out over the cloth at the back. Push a coin up under the center of the clip so it is held tightly, and let the bottom edge of your jacket fall into place to cover it.

Now let's suppose you come to the part of some trick where you want to get the coin secretly into your right hand. Just let your hand hang naturally at your right side, and momentarily turn your left side toward those watching. Curl your right fingers up under the edge of the jacket, pull the coin from the clip, loosely close your fingers to hide the coin in them, and let your hand drop to your side before you face front again.

If the particular trick allows for it, you should be showing your viewers something in your left hand as you steal the clipped coin with the right hand.

A pen-clip holder set up in the outside corner of the *left* back pocket can be used to get a coin or some other object into the *left* hand in the same way.

If you are not wearing a jacket, but are wearing a sweater or a loose shirt that comes down outside your slacks, the pen clip can still be used in a back pocket. But check first to make sure the bottom edge of the sweater or shirt covers whatever you have in the clip.

Secretly Adding Cards to a Pack

To add a card (or cards) secretly to the *top* of a pack, have the card vertical and *face outward* in the clip. Hold the pack vertically between your thumb at one side edge and fingers around the other side edge, with the *back* of the pack toward your body as you drop your hand to your side.

As you momentarily turn your other side toward those watching, bring the pack up under the edge of the jacket against the clipped card, grip the side edges of it between thumb and fingers, and let your hand drop to your side again, with the card in place on the pack.

To add a card to the *face* of the pack, have it clipped *back outward*, and hold the pack *facing your body*. (This is a good way to secretly add a double-faced card [see page 157] to a borrowed pack.)

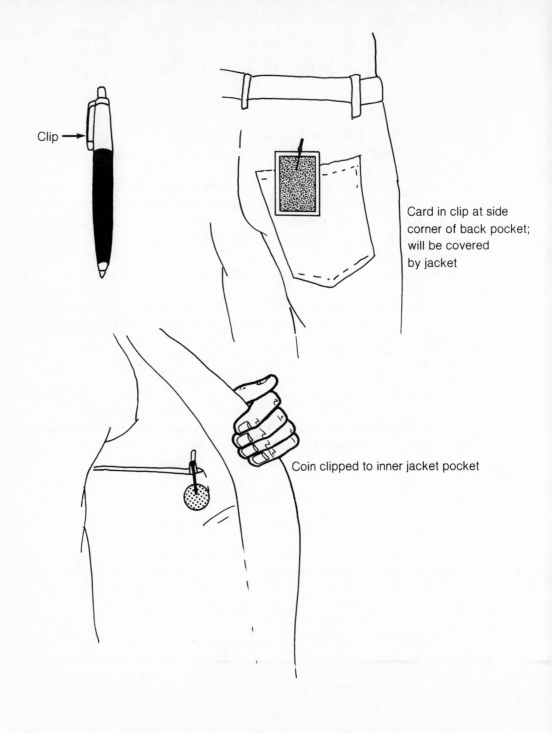

Clip

Card in clip at side
corner of back pocket;
will be covered
by jacket

Coin clipped to inner jacket pocket

Using the Pen Clip to Switch Things

Because the pen part down inside the pocket holds the pocket open at the top corner, it is easy to use the pocket and clip to switch things without fumbling to get your fingers into the pocket.

Let's say you have a half-dollar in your hand that you want to switch secretly for a quarter that is hidden under the clip. Let your hand fall to your side for a moment, as before, and as you turn that side of your body away slightly, curl your fingers up under the jacket edge. Drop the half-dollar into the open top of the pocket, pull the clipped quarter into your fingers, and let your hand fall to your side again.

With Things Held behind Your Back

If you want to use the clip during some trick in which you hold something in your hands behind your back, fasten the pen to the top edge of either pocket at the *inner* corner, rather than the outside corner, so it will be easier to reach.

In the Inside Jacket Pocket

The pen clip can be used in much the same way in the inside left or right breast pocket of your jacket. But there must be some good reason for openly reaching into the pocket, such as to take out the pen, an envelope, or a folded sheet of paper that you have there. The pen should be clipped to the top edge at the *center* of the pocket, instead of at the corner. Whatever is hidden under the clip is held by it against the *outside* of the pocket.

Suppose again that you secretly want to add to the pack a card that is clipped to the inside right pocket. With the pack held in your left hand, you might say, for instance, "For this, we will also need an envelope."

Taking the front edge of the jacket with your right hand to hold it open a little, you would reach in under your jacket with your left hand, quickly add the clipped card to the pack, and bring the pack out again, along with the envelope that was in the pocket.

To switch a coin in your hand for another clipped to your inside pocket, you might say you would like someone to write down the date of the coin. Then reach in under your jacket, drop the coin from your hand into the pocket, get the clipped coin, and bring out the pen.

Inside a Purse

A purse that has a small pocket attached to its inside lining can be used with a pen-clip holder in much the same way as an inside jacket pocket. Use only the *cap* of the pen. Put the cap into the little lining pocket, with the clip attached to the center of the pocket's top edge, so the clip comes down over the outside of the pocket.

You can have a coin, key, folded dollar bill, or other small flat object clipped there and held apart from other things that may be in the purse. As you reach into the purse to bring out something else that is part of the particular trick you happen to be doing, you can quickly and secretly get the clipped object hidden in your fingers before you bring your hand out again.

Slit Envelopes

An ordinary envelope can be made very quickly into one for vanishing a coin, key, ring, folded dollar bill, or other small object, simply by slitting open one edge.

By having one or two of these easily prepared envelopes in an inside jacket pocket or a purse, along with a few letters or memos, you can make your decision to use one seem impromptu, as if you just happened to think of using it at that moment.

You might make some remark about needing an envelope, take the papers from your pocket or purse, toss the prepared envelope out on the table, and say offhandedly, "I guess this will do." If you wish, you can have some notes or figures scribbled on the back of it, as if that were the reason for having it with you.

Side-Slit Envelope

This is used mainly for vanishing a coin, key, or ring. One *side edge* is slit open, so that when the envelope is held between the hands and tilted, whatever has been put into it secretly slides out through the slit into your fingers.

To prepare the envelope, turn it back upward, and with a sharp pair of scissors cut just a tiny sliver off the *left* side edge, from the bottom

Side-Slit Envelope

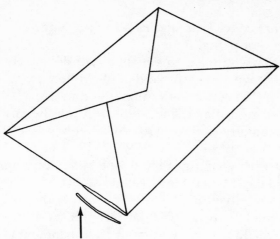

Tiny sliver cut off edge

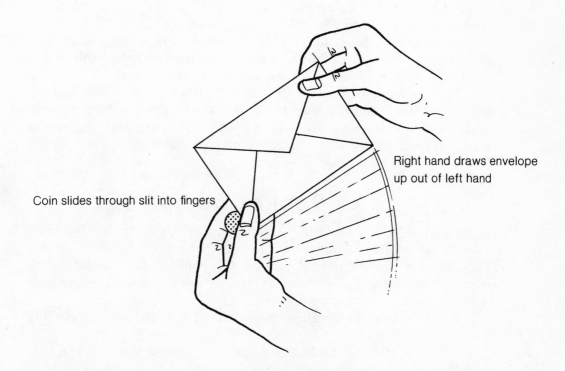

Coin slides through slit into fingers

Right hand draws envelope up out of left hand

corner up to the center of that edge. Trim off just a hairline edge of the paper, only enough to leave that part slit open.

Suppose, for instance, that you want to vanish a half-dollar. Hold the back-upward envelope flat with the left hand at the bottom left corner, fingers under the side of that corner and thumb on top.

Show the coin with your right hand, and place it inside the envelope. Lift the envelope horizontally upright with your left hand, so the coin falls to the bottom of it.

Fold down the top flap with your right hand, and slide your right thumb and fingers along the flap to take the envelope at its upper right corner. As you do that, tilt the envelope slightly between both hands, sliding the coin down into the left corner and out through the slit into your left fingers. Draw the envelope away with your right hand, and let your left hand fall to your side with the coin hidden in it.

You can get rid of the coin by reaching into a left-hand pocket to leave it there as you bring out something else that is part of whatever trick you happen to be doing.

When you are ready to show that the half-dollar has vanished from the envelope, open the flap, and hold that with your right hand as you put your left fingers down into the top of the envelope at the left side.

Turn the envelope mouth downward, pulling it open and shaking it upside down to indicate that it is empty. Then quickly pull your hands apart to rip the envelope open along the left side edge, and continue to tear it apart until the whole inside is opened out. Finally crumple the envelope, and toss it aside.

The Pocket Dumper

With this method of using the side-slit envelope, you can vanish whatever is put into it without having to slide it out secretly into your fingers. There is no need to hide the object in your hand, or to make some excuse to get rid of it. The object drops right out of the envelope to hide itself in one of your pockets.

You will need an envelope that is slit open at the lower *right* side edge.

To use it, turn the back of the envelope toward you. Lift the flap, and hold that between your first and second left fingers, with your thumb down inside to keep the back of the envelope opened out.

Show the coin with your right hand, hold it a few inches above the envelope, and drop the coin so that it visibly falls down into the envelope.

The Pocket Dumper

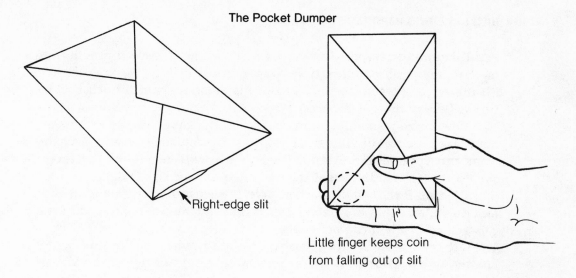

Right-edge slit

Little finger keeps coin
from falling out of slit

Envelope held end up to put into pocket

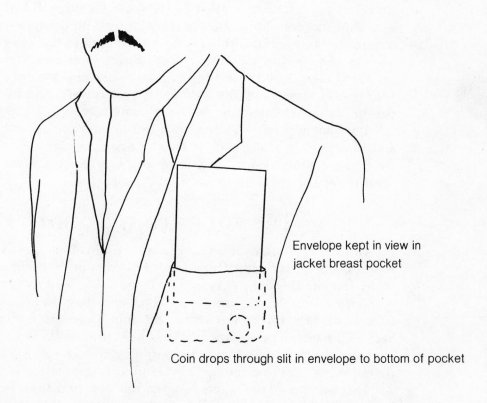

Envelope kept in view in
jacket breast pocket

Coin drops through slit in envelope to bottom of pocket

Take the envelope between both hands, lift it to your mouth, lick the flap, and seal it by pressing your thumbs across it. As you do that, tilt the envelope slightly so the coin inside slides into the *left* bottom corner (where there is no slit).

Now move your right hand up, so that the envelope's top right corner is at the center of your right palm, with your fingers down over the front and your thumb extended over the back. The right little finger should rest against the slit at the envelope's lower right edge.

Holding it that way, take the envelope with the right hand, turn it face down, and slap the free end of it on the table, so the sound of the coin sealed inside it can be heard.

Lift the envelope upright again, on end, with the slit end at the bottom, where your little finger and the pressure of your thumb keep the coin from sliding out.

"I'll put the envelope right here, so you can keep an eye on it," you say, as you put the bottom end down inside the outer breast pocket, or right side pocket, of your jacket. Let the coin secretly fall from the envelope into the bottom of the pocket, and leave the envelope standing upright in the pocket, with most of it remaining in full view.

Go on with the rest of your trick, until you are ready to show that the coin has vanished from the envelope. Then pull the envelope out of your pocket, turn it lengthwise with its back toward you, and tear open part of the sealed flap at the top right corner.

Put your right first finger down inside the envelope at that corner and run it down to the bottom, tearing open the right edge. Then run your finger along inside the bottom edge to tear the whole envelope open wide, and show there is nothing inside.

Disappearing Dollar

For vanishing a dollar bill, you can use an envelope that is slit at the center of its *bottom* edge. Cut a very tiny edge off the bottom, directly under the middle of the envelope, to make a slit about two inches wide.

Borrow a dollar bill, fold it twice in half lengthwise, and take the folded bill at the top between your left thumb and first finger. Turn the back of the envelope toward you, and hold it flat with your right hand at the center of the bottom edge, gripping it between the tip of your thumb at the back and the tips of your four fingers at the front.

Use your free left fingers to open the flap, and then slide the bill halfway down inside the middle of the envelope. Take your left hand

Disappearing Dollar

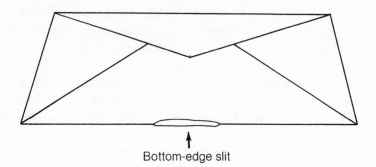

Bottom-edge slit

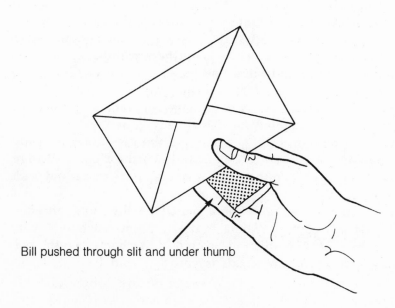

Bill pushed through slit and under thumb

away for a moment, press your right thumb against the bottom of the bill through the envelope, and turn the envelope around so everyone can see the bill that is partway down inside it.

Bring the flap side toward you again, holding the envelope upright. With your left hand, push the bill all the way down into the envelope and through the slit at the bottom, so the lower end of the bill comes out beneath your right thumb. With that thumb, press the bill against the inside of your upright fingers. Because of the position of your hand holding the envelope, the bill is hidden from front view.

Raise the envelope to your mouth, lick the flap, and seal the envelope by running your left thumb over the flap. With your left hand, grip the left edge of the envelope. Lift the envelope up out of your right hand, leaving the bill hidden behind your right fingers.

Immediately reach with your right hand, the bill concealed in it, into one of your right-hand pockets, and leave the bill in it as you bring something else out of the pocket to show it.

You might have a pencil in your pocket, for example, and bring that out as you ask the lender of the bill if he or she remembers the serial number of the dollar, so you can write it on the envelope. The answer will be that the person doesn't know the number, since you didn't ask that it be looked at it when you borrowed the bill.

"That's too bad," you say. "I'm sorry we have no record of it because I'm afraid you've lost your money. . . . It's already gone!"

Tear open the right corner of the flap, put the pencil down inside, and slit the envelope open with the pencil, down the right side edge, then across the bottom and up the other side edge, to open it out wide and show it is empty.

Drop the opened-out envelope and pencil on the table, and also show your hands are empty. Wait a moment, then reach into your pocket, quickly open out the bill, and bring it out to hand it to the person, as you say, "I don't know if this is yours. . . . But I know it isn't mine."

Rubber Band Pulls

A *pull* is a device magicians use to pull something secretly from the hand up the sleeve or in under the jacket. You can easily make simple pulls for use with your impromptu magic by stringing together two ordinary rubber bands. Each pull will also need a small safety pin at one end, to fasten it into place.

Where you fasten the pull and what you attach to the other end will depend on how you want to use it. You might attach a coin, key, paper clip, ring, candy LifeSaver, or a coat button, to vanish the thing itself— or attach a small bulldog clip to grip a variety of other things with it, and make those disappear.

Up the Sleeve

You can accomplish some really puzzling coin vanishes with a quarter attached to a sleeve pull. By wearing the pull pinned in your sleeve, you can seem to take the quarter out of your pocket, and vanish it whenever you wish.

To rig it up, you will need two rubber bands, each about three inches long, the small safety pin, a quarter, and transparent tape.

Hitch the two bands together end to end by looping one through the other and bringing the loop down over the first one so the two are knotted. Attach the safety pin to the free end of the first band by pushing the doubled end up through the small hole at the bottom of the pin, and bringing that loop up over the top of the pin and back down to the bottom again.

Take a strip of tape about an inch and a half long, and stick one end across the back of the quarter. Place the free end of the rubber band on the tape, right against the edge of the coin. Bend the tape up through the band and then down across the face of the quarter. (The tape won't show because it is transparent. It should be replaced with a fresh strip after it has been used several times, to avoid having the rubber band unexpectedly tear through it. Just peel off the old tape and stick on a new one.)

Now remove your jacket, and fasten the safety pin to your right sleeve at the inside of the arm just opposite the elbow. Hold the quarter in your right hand, and put the jacket on again. When you release the quarter, it should hang hidden inside your jacket sleeve about two inches up from the bottom edge.

The sleeve pull can be used with any small flat object instead of the coin. If what you attach has a hole in it, such as a key or ring, there is no need to use the tape. Just push the end of the rubber band up through the hole, and loop the band down over it.

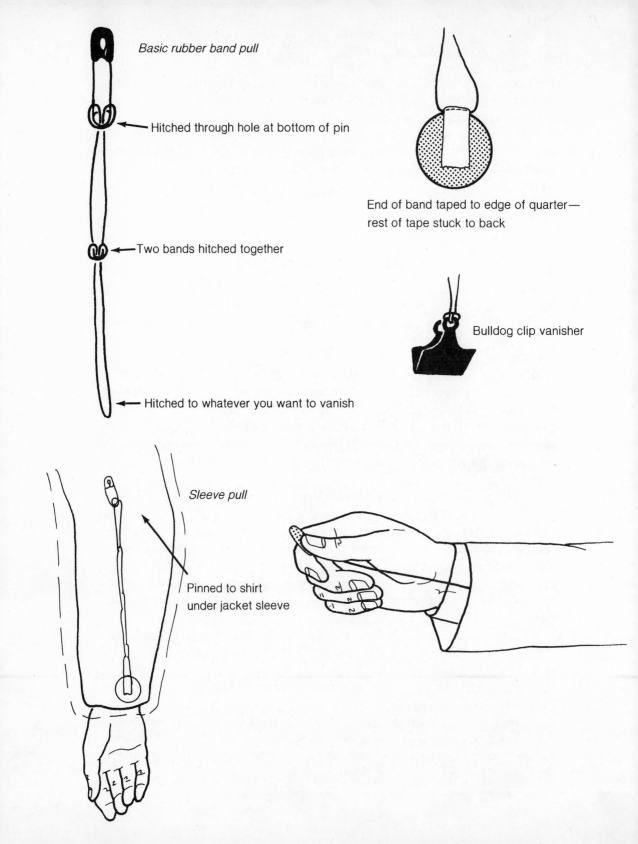

Basic rubber band pull

Hitched through hole at bottom of pin

Two bands hitched together

Hitched to whatever you want to vanish

End of band taped to edge of quarter—
rest of tape stuck to back

Bulldog clip vanisher

Sleeve pull

Pinned to shirt
under jacket sleeve

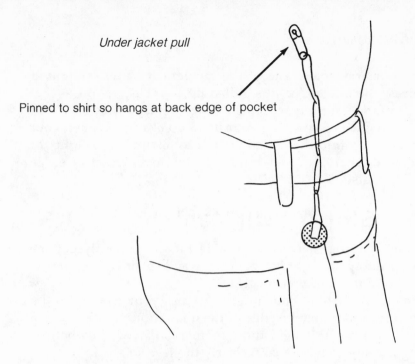

Under jacket pull

Pinned to shirt so hangs at back edge of pocket

Toss-Up Vanish

Have the quarter-attached pull pinned in your sleeve, and some loose change in your right pants or skirt pocket.

Just before you are ready to do the trick, stand with both hands clasped behind your back for a moment. Secretly reach up inside your right sleeve with your left fingers, and pull the attached quarter down into your right hand. Hold it against the inside of your right fingers with your thumb.

Put your hand into your pocket, jingle the loose change, and push the quarter to the tips of your first two fingers, keeping it held with your thumb at the attached edge. The rubber band runs through your other two partly closed fingers and up behind your wrist into the sleeve, so it will be hidden from front view.

Bring out the quarter as though you had taken it from the loose change in your pocket, and show it at your fingertips, with the back of your hand toward those watching.

"You've probably heard of the floating lady illusion," you say. "But did you ever see George Washington float through the air? That's what the Washington on this quarter is about to to do."

Slowly swing your arm down to your side and then back up, as if you were about to toss the quarter into the air, but don't let go of it yet.

Again swing your arm down, and at the moment it hangs straight at your side, release the quarter, so it is pulled up your sleeve.

Keep your thumb and fingers pinched together as if they still held the quarter, and immediately swing your hand up again and open your fingers wide. Look up into the air, as though following the "flight" of the coin, and say, "There he goes—and like the floating lady, George Washington has vanished in mid-air!"

Slap-Down Vanish

You need to be standing in front of a table for this. Secretly get the attached quarter into your right hand, in the way explained previously, and pretend to take it out of your pocket.

Show the quarter held at your fingertips, turn your hand with the fingers downward, and strike the edge of the quarter on the table so the sound can be heard. Keep it held there momentarily, with its bottom edge touching the table, and the coin clearly in view.

"I don't know if it's true," you say, "but I've heard you can bend a quarter if you strike it down hard enough, at just the right angle."

Lower your hand to your side, bring it back up, and strike the edge of the quarter on the table again. Shake your head, make some remark about not striking it hard enough, and lower your hand to your side again. As you do, release the quarter so it goes up your sleeve, but keep your thumb and fingers pinched together as if they still held it, and bring your hand up over the table once more.

This time strike your fingers down hard, and quickly open them out flat so your palm slaps the table. Lift your hand slowly to reveal that the quarter has disappeared, and say, "*Too* hard that time. . . . I scared it away."

Catch as Catch Can

Pretend to take the attached quarter out of your pocket. Hold it up to show it at your right fingertips, and say to someone, "Here's a little stunt that will test your reflexes. Hold out your hand like this."

You show the person by holding out your own left hand, flat and palm up, in front of you. "I'm going to drop this quarter into your hand." Turn your right hand over, fingers down, and tap the quarter against *your* flat left palm. "As soon as I drop it, close your fingers around it."

Lift your right hand with the quarter, and then lower that arm slightly as you quickly close your left fingers, demonstrating what he or she is to do. Look at your left hand, and then at the person, and say, "That looks easy, doesn't it? Remember to close your fingers quickly."

As you speak, release the quarter so it is drawn up your sleeve, but keep your right thumb and fingers pinched together as if they still held the coin. Open your *left* hand, let it fall to your side, and ask, "Do you understand?"

Bring your right hand a few inches above the person's hand. Say, "Ready? . . . Catch!" Open your fingers as though dropping the quarter.

The person usually will close his or her hand while trying to catch the coin, before realizing that it has vanished, and there is no quarter. Whether or not that happens, open your hand wide to show it is empty. Bring up your empty left hand, look first at one hand and then the other, and then look at the person and ask, "What did you do with it?"

Bulldog Clip Vanisher

This simple device can be used to make all sorts of small things disappear by secretly pulling them in under your jacket.

The device can be used openly, by seeming to take it from your pocket and showing it as you clip it to something, or it can be kept hidden in your fingers, and secretly clipped to whatever you want to vanish.

You will need a small (size "0") bulldog clip, commonly available at stationery stores. It has strong clamplike jaws that grip tightly, and is only about an inch in width and length.

Attach the clip to a pull made of two rubber bands by pushing the free end of the bottom band through the hole in one of the handles of the clip, and then bringing that looped end down over the clip.

Fasten the safety pin to the right side seam of your shirt or blouse about an inch above your belt. The clip should hang down at the top back edge of your pants or skirt pocket, where it will be covered by your jacket. Put the dangling clip just inside the top of that pocket.

Suppose that you want to vanish the torn-up pieces of a card or a slip of paper. Hold the pieces in view with your left hand and turn your left side slightly toward those watching as you say, "I'll clip these together."

Reach to your pocket with your right hand. Get the handles of the clip between your thumb and first finger, and close your other fingers around the attached rubber band. As you face front, push your hand down into the pocket, as if reaching into the bottom of it to find the clip.

Take the clip out to show it, with the back of your hand toward those watching, and move your hand over in front of your waist. Lean a little forward from your waist, so your jacket will fall back into place and hang open at the front and away from your body. (At this point, the stretched rubber band runs through the inside of your right fingers and behind your wrist up under your jacket, so it is hidden from view by your hand and arm.)

Now bring your left hand over with the torn pieces. Press open the clip with your right thumb, and fasten it to the pieces. Turn your left hand palm upward in front of you, and place the clip on the left palm, still holding its attached end between your right thumb and finger. Slowly close your left fingers up around it, and *gently* release the clip so it is drawn back through your right fingers and pulled under your jacket.

Keep your left hand closed, as though it still held the clip, and tap that hand with your right one. Move both hands forward, away from your body, show your right hand is empty, and slowly open your left hand to show that the clip and the torn pieces have disappeared.

In the same way, you might vanish a dollar bill, after folding it twice in half in each direction, and then bringing out the clip to fasten it to the bill.

Again, you might "discover" some loose postage or trading stamps in one of your pockets, remark that you had better keep them together so they won't get lost, bring out the clip to hold them, and pretend to be surprised when the stamps and clip disappear.

With the Clip Hidden

The bulldog clip pull is more useful for vanishing many other things if it is kept hidden in the hand instead of being openly clipped to the objects. For example, here's how you might make a stick of chewing gum disappear:

Have the gum in your left pants or skirt pocket and the pull-attached clip hanging just inside the top of the right pocket. Put both hands into your pockets, as if searching in them for the stick of gum, and turn your left side slightly toward those watching. Take the gum out of your left pocket to show it as you get the clip hidden in your right fingers, holding the clip with your thumb inside the fingertips, so the thumb can easily press the clip open.

Face front as you bring both hands together close to your body and below your waist. With your left hand, put one end of the stick of gum into the clip hidden in the right hand, as though transferring the gum from the fingertips of one hand to the other.

Close your left hand into a loose fist, and pretend to push the free end of the gum down into the top of it with your right hand. But really slide the right fingers down along the gum, and release the pull so it is secretly drawn through the right hand and back under your jacket.

Keep the left fist closed, as if it held the gum, and hold the fist away from you. Look at that hand, rub the fingers together, and slowly open it to show that the gum has vanished. Then casually show that your right hand also is empty.

You might vanish a short pencil by secretly gripping the end of it with the hidden clip—or vanish a typewriter eraser, a stick pretzel, a cigarette, a small bunch of wooden matches or toothpicks.

Two stacked-together coins or poker chips can be secretly gripped by the clip while transferring them from the fingertips of one hand to the other.

A facial tissue can be shown, crumpled into a tight little ball, and vanished by pinching part of the tissue in the hidden clip. The clip will also take a packet of book matches.

In all these vanishes, remember to keep your right hand close to the edge of your jacket, so the pull doesn't travel far. Release it *gently*, letting it inch back through your fingers, and *after* you release it, pretend that the thing you have shown is still in your hands. Creating the illusion that it is still in your hands, after it secretly has been pulled under your jacket, makes the vanish convincing.

Double-Faced Cards

Double-faced cards have a face on both sides instead of a face and a back. Since they have no back designs, a double-faced card can be secretly added to a borrowed pack, from which you secretly remove it before returning the pack to its owner.

With one or two such cards you can accomplish some rather startling tricks that otherwise would require expert sleight of hand. They

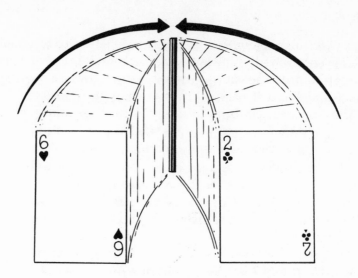

Two of your own cards glued together back to back so there are faces on both sides

have an extra advantage in that people aren't as likely to suspect the use of trick cards in a borrowed pack as they might be if you were using a pack of your own.

Specially printed double-faced cards are available at magic shops, and at some joke and novelty counters. But you can very easily make a few from an old pack of ordinary cards. Simply choose the two faces you want to use for a particular trick, and fasten those two cards together back to back to make the double-faced card.

A stick adhesive, such as Glue-Stick, probably is the best to use, or you can stick the cards together with white craft glue or rubber cement. Coat the entire back of each card, especially around the edges, and make sure all the edges are exactly matched and firmly pressed together.

Usually it is a good idea to do a trick or two with the borrowed pack, so others can shuffle the cards and handle them, before you secretly add the double-facer.

You can have that special card in a pocket, and, after you finish some other trick, put the pack into your pocket for a moment as if to free your hands to do something else—to pick something up, to clear more space on the table, to hitch your chair in closer. Then bring the pack out again with the double-faced card added to the face of it.

After you finish using the pack, you can get rid of the double-faced card by "absentmindedly" putting the pack back into your pocket, just long enough to drop the extra card and leave it there. Then take out the pack again and hand it back to its owner, with some remark such as, "Sorry. They *are* your cards, aren't they? I didn't mean to walk off with them."

Here are some tricks that show various uses of a double-faced card with a borrowed pack.

The One-Eyed King

HOW IT LOOKS

"Have you ever noticed that the king of diamonds is a one-eyed king?" you ask, as you show the king on the face of the pack. "All the other kings have two eyes, but he has only one. Legend has it that when the king of diamonds first looked at his queen, he was half blinded by her beauty. I don't know about that, but he does seem to be devoted to her."

You take the king from the face of the pack, and slowly push it into the middle of the face-up pack. Turning the pack face down, you quickly spread the cards out across the table, and the queen of diamonds appears face up. "He always has his eye on her whenever she turns up."

Removing the queen, you gather up the pack, and say, "She seems to be as devoted to him." You push the queen into the middle of the pack. "She's always waiting anxiously for him to appear." Again you spread the cards out face down, and now the king appears face up among them. "There he is again—his royal highness, the one-eyed king."

THE SET-UP

Make a double-faced king of diamonds–queen of diamonds. Secretly add it to the face of the borrowed pack, with the king side to the front.

WHAT YOU DO

Hold the pack face down, and casually spread the cards between your hands to show their backs, but be careful not to expose the double-faced card at the bottom. Square the pack, turn it over face up, and show the "one-eyed king" on the face of it.

Remove the king, keeping the card flat, and slowly push it face up into the middle of the face-up pack. Turn the pack over, and spread the face-down cards across the table in a long overlapping row. The queen (really the reverse side of the king) appears face up at the center of the spread.

Slide the queen out on the table, gather up the pack, and turn it face up. Slowly push the face-up queen into the middle of the pack. Turn the pack face down, and spread out the cards as before. The king (really the reverse side of the queen) now appears face up.

Two-Card Find the Lady

HOW IT LOOKS

You remove a queen of spades and a ten of diamonds from the pack, and explain that you are about to demonstrate a version of the old street corner gambling game called Find the Lady. "But instead of the usual three cards," you say, "I'll use only two—just to make it easier for you."

You hold up both cards to show them separately, slowly bring them together, turn them over several times to show both sides, and spread them apart on the table with the ten face up and the queen face down.

Then you invite someone to place a hand over the card he or she thinks is the queen. "You can hardly miss," you say. "Just put your hand on it and keep it there."

The person puts his or her hand over the face-down card, and you pick up the ten of diamonds and push that into the pack. But when the card thought to be the queen is turned over, it has changed to the ten of diamonds.

You spread out the face-down pack, and the missing queen of spades is face up at the center of it!

THE SET-UP

You will need a double-faced queen of spades–ten of diamonds. Secretly add the card to the face of the borrowed pack, with the queen side showing.

WHAT YOU DO

Place the pack face up on the table. Slide off the double-faced queen, and lay that on the table. Pick up the pack, quickly look through it, remove the ten of diamonds, and place that card face up on the table beside the queen. Put the face-up pack aside.

Pick up the ten of diamonds with your left thumb and first finger, and hold it upright and close to you, its face to the front and its back

Two-Card Find the Lady

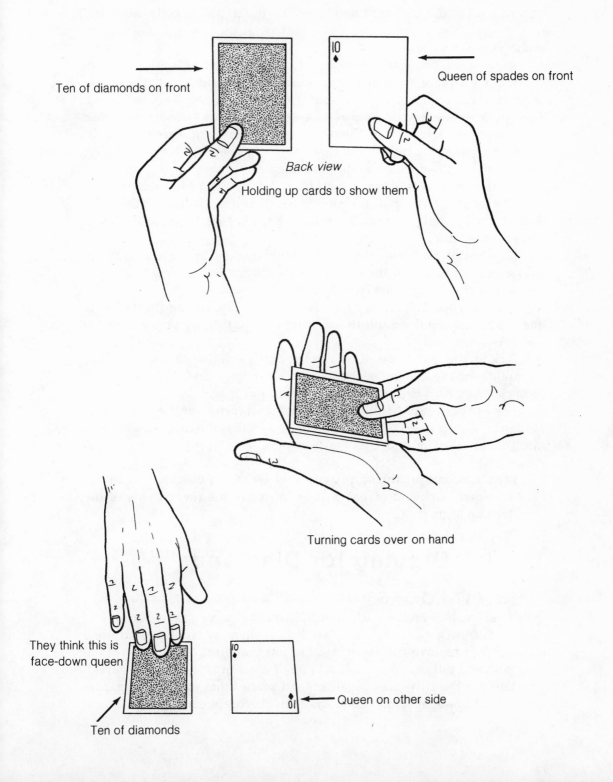

Ten of diamonds on front

Queen of spades on front

Back view

Holding up cards to show them

Turning cards over on hand

They think this is face-down queen

Ten of diamonds

Queen on other side

toward you. With your right hand, pick up the double-faced queen, and hold it close to you the same way, apart from the other, being careful not to expose its back.

Very slowly, bring the two cards toward each other, with the *queen in front*, and square them together. Lower your hands, and slowly rest the two cards together on the outstretched fingers of your left hand. Turn them over together from *right to left*, spread the two apart on your hand to show them, square them up as they were, and turn them over together from *left to right*. Now turn them together, *end over end*, twice, and put them down together on the table.

Distract attention for a moment from the relative position of the two cards by saying, "The point of the game, of course, is to find the lady. Since there are only two cards, you can hardly miss." Spread the cards apart on the table.

(The ten of diamonds side of the double-faced card is now face up, so it seems obvious that the face-down card must be the queen, but it is really the ten of diamonds from the pack.)

Ask someone to place a hand over the card he or she thinks is the queen and to keep the hand there. The person naturally puts a hand on the face-down card.

Pick up the double-faced ten, and openly push that card face up into the middle of the face-up pack on the table, being careful not to expose its back. Then turn the pack *face down*, and put it aside.

Ask the person to lift his or her hand, and turn over the card surely thought to be the queen. The person discovers that the card has changed into the ten of diamonds that you were just seen putting back into the pack.

Wait a second for the surprise to register. Then quickly spread out the face-down pack and reveal the queen (really the reverse side of the ten), face up at its center.

Digging for Diamonds

HOW IT LOOKS

"We're about to search for diamonds," you say, as you take the nine of diamonds from a pack of cards. "To dig for them, we'll also need some spades." You remove the five of spades, put that on the table next to the first card, and put the pack aside. "Nine of diamonds . . . five of spades."

You put the two cards together, and place them under a magazine or a folded newspaper on the table. "Now before we start our exploration, do you mind if I test your sense of direction?" you ask. "I wouldn't want you to think that I tried to swindle you out of the diamonds."

Reaching under the magazine, you slide out the nine of diamonds, pick it up, and openly put it into your jacket pocket. Then you ask where each card is. The answer, of course, is that the diamond card is in your pocket, and the spade card is under the magazine. "That's right," you say. "I'm glad you're watching closely."

You place both cards together under the magazine again. "This time, I'll take away the spades." Sliding out the five of spades, you pick it up, and openly put it into your jacket pocket. "Now where is the nine of diamonds?"

When they answer that it is under the magazine, you shake your head, and say, "No. I'm afraid you're wrong. *I've* got the diamonds." You take the nine of diamonds out of your pocket and drop it on the table. "And that leaves you with the spades." You lift the magazine, and show the five of spades.

THE SET-UP

Have a nine of diamonds–five of spades double-faced card in the right-hand pocket of your jacket, with the nine side of the card to the front. You will need to borrow an old magazine or a folded newspaper, which you place flat on the table.

WHAT YOU DO

Look through the pack, and remove first the nine of diamonds and then the five of spades, and put the pack aside.

Call attention to each of the cards by name, and place the nine on top of the five. Hold the two together at their bottom edge between your right thumb and first finger, and, with your left hand, lift the back of the magazine enough so your right hand can put the cards under the center of it.

Explain to those watching that you want to test their "sense of direction." Reach under the magazine with your right hand, and slide out the top card, the nine of diamonds. Pick it up, keeping the face of it to the front, and openly put it into your jacket pocket, down behind the double-faced card that is hidden there.

Ask which card is still under the magazine, and when they answer that it is the five of spades, say, "That's right. I'm glad you're watching closely."

Slide the five of spades out from under the magazine, and leave it on the table. Then reach into your pocket again and take out the *front* card, the double-faced nine–five. Keep its nine side toward the front, and be careful not to expose its back as you place the card on the table next to the five of spades. (This looks as if you are taking the same nine from your pocket that you previously put there.)

Now you seem to do what you did before. But as you put the two cards together on the table, leave the fake nine *face up,* and place the five *face down* on top of it so they are face to face.

Again hold the two flat together between your right thumb and fingers at the bottom edge, and, with your left hand, lift the back of the magazine enough to put the cards under the center of it. But as your right hand goes under the magazine, just turn that hand over, right to left, to turn the cards over together as you leave them under the magazine.

"This time, I'll take away the spades," you say. Reach under the magazine and slide out the top card, the double-faced one with its five of spades side now face up. Pick it up, keeping its face to the front, and openly put it into your pocket, down behind the nine of diamonds that is hidden there. Remove your hand, and ask, "Now where is the nine of diamonds?"

They answer that it is under the magazine, but you say, "No. I'm afraid you're wrong. *I've* got the diamonds." You pull the front card out of your pocket, the nine of diamonds, and drop it on the table. "And that leaves you with the spades." You lift away the magazine and show the five of spades.

(The double-faced card remains hidden in your pocket, as it was at the start of the trick, and the two cards on the table are the ordinary ones that you took from the borrowed pack.)

Sticky Stuff

A small pellet of puttylike adhesive, usually no bigger than the head of a match, is among the most useful secret aids for all sorts of impromptu magic.

With it, you can stick cards or coins together, attach them to other things, temporarily fasten them to your fingers, or hide them in other places. Thread can be secretly hitched to various objects. A pen, pencil, soda straw, knife, spoon, or paper cup can be made to cling to the fingertips or elsewhere, seeming to defy gravity.

Magicians have found endless uses for an adhesive known as *magicians' wax*, sold by magic shops. It is as tacky as chewing gum, sticks instantly, and yet can be quickly detached. But there are several other substances that work as well and that are available at variety and stationery stores, in gift shops, and in many supermarkets.

Among the best for magical purposes is a blue putty-type adhesive marketed under the brand name of Fun-Tak. It is packaged in flat strips shaped like thick sticks of chewing gum. You break off as much as you need, and roll it in your fingers until it becomes soft and tacky. It will stick to just about any smooth or hard surface, remains sticky, and is easily removed.

Substances known as *candle adhesives,* made to keep candles upright in their holders, can also be used. These are soft, white, waxlike adhesives, much the same as magicians' wax, and come packaged in small metal containers. You scrape out the amount you need, and roll it into a tacky pellet.

Chewing gum itself, a tiny piece that has been well chewed, allowed to dry, and then kneaded with the fingers, can also be used for spur-of-the-moment trickery, but the other adhesives are much better.

If you stick a little pellet of adhesive to the *back* of the lower front button of your jacket, you can have it ready to use whenever you want it. By turning away for a moment, you can secretly scrape it off the button with a fingernail or the tip of a finger.

Another good place to have the adhesive is at the back of one of your jacket sleeve buttons, at either the left or right side. Folding your arms across in front of you puts it at your fingertips.

If you aren't wearing a jacket, stick the adhesive to the back of a cuff button of your shirt, or, if one of the rear pockets of your slacks has a button, you can have it there.

You may prefer to have a bit of it stuck to the face of a half-dollar you carry in a pants or skirt pocket, or fastened to a small square of cardboard in one of your other pockets. A pellet can be stuck to the top of a pen clipped into one of your inside jacket pockets, so you can scrape it off with a fingernail as you take out the pen.

It can be stuck to the back of a pad of paper, a notebook or wallet, to the outside of the cardboard case, if you are using your own pack of cards, to a pocket lighter, or a matchbook. If you are setting things up in advance, you can have it already in place on one of the props for the trick.

Here are some tricks that show various ways it can be used.

Sure Thing

Stick a tiny bit of adhesive to the back of a dime, and have that and a nickel in a right-hand pocket. Take them out and lay them next to each other on your outstretched left fingers, with the dime's sticky side down.

"Two coins," you say, as you pick up the dime and put it on top of the nickel, secretly pressing it so they stick together. "A nickel and a dime."

Close your left fingers, which automatically turns the coins *over* into your palm, and leaves the nickel uppermost. Lift your closed left hand so the little finger is at the bottom, and bring it down to your held-out right hand. Open your left fingers just enough to let the nickel (with the attached dime hidden beneath it) slide out into your right palm. Immediately lift your closed left hand away, as though it still held the dime, and hold that hand out in front of you.

Display the nickel lying on your open right palm, and flatly jiggle it around a bit. "One coin in each hand." Slowly close your right fingers, and ask, "Which hand holds the nickel?" Since you just showed it there, the answer will be that it is in your right hand. "That's right," you say, as you open your right hand and show the nickel again. "Now I'm going to give you a chance to bet on an absolutely sure thing."

You put the nickel away in your pocket (with the attached dime), bring your right hand out to show it is empty, and extend your still-closed left hand.

"I'll bet you a dime that you can't guess which hand the dime is in," you say. "But before I take your bet, there's something I'd better tell you. . . ." Slowly open your left hand, and show that the dime has vanished. "I haven't got a dime to pay you if you win."

Half Vanished

Attach a pellet of adhesive to a half-dollar, and have that in one of your pockets with a nickel, a quarter, and a business card.

Take out the card and place it lengthwise on your left palm, then bring out each of the coins, and lay them on the card in a row, secretly pressing the half-dollar so it sticks to the card.

Half Vanished

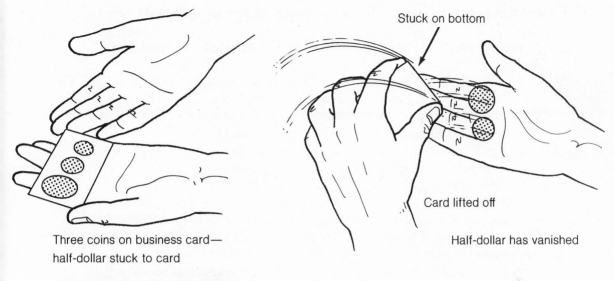

Stuck on bottom

Card lifted off

Three coins on business card—
half-dollar stuck to card

Half-dollar has vanished

Card is tipped over upside down to
cover coins spilled into right hand

"A nickel, a quarter, and a half-dollar," you say. Hold out your right hand, and tip the card over to spill the coins into your right palm, dropping the turned-over card on top of them so they lie covered by it. (The half-dollar remains stuck to what is now the underside of the card.) "If you had your choice of one of them," you ask someone, "which would you choose?"

The person usually will say the half-dollar. Take the card by its long edges between your left thumb and first finger, keep it flat, and lift it off your right hand to reveal that the half-dollar has vanished, and that only the nickel and quarter remain on your right palm.

"You called it," you say, "and it's gone!" (If the person happened to choose one of the other coins, just say instead, "I'm glad you didn't want the half-dollar, because that's already gone.")

In either case, lay the nickel and quarter back on top of the card to show them, keeping the card held in the same position with your left hand, and also show that your right hand is empty. Bring your right hand to the card to take the coins again, by putting your thumb over them and your fingers under the card.

As your thumb pulls the nickel and quarter off the top, scoop your right fingers along under the card to pull the half-dollar secretly away with them, and immediately close your right fingers around all the coins.

With your left hand, drop the card to the table or tuck it into a pocket.

Jingle the coins in your closed right hand, and say, "But the half-dollar has only *half vanished*. It hasn't really disappeared." Open your right hand, and show the three coins on your palm. "It was just a little shy, but now it's back again."

Beats the Band

Someone chooses a card from a borrowed pack, puts it back, and you cut the cards several times to mix them, and place the pack on the table. You take a rubber band out of your pocket, hand it to the person, and ask him to put the band around the pack.

Then you grip the two ends of the rubber band, hold the dangling pack upright above the table, and ask the person to call out the name of his or her card. As that is done, you stretch the band to release the cards so they all fall out to the table, except for one. The chosen card hangs facing the person inside the encircling rubber band!

You will need a flat rubber band that will fit snugly around a pack of cards. Have it in your right-hand jacket pocket with a small piece of cardboard that has a pellet of adhesive on it.

Borrow a pack of cards, and ask someone to choose one card. Have the person show it to the others who are watching, without letting you see it, and return it to the pack.

Secretly bring it to the top, using the method explained in Chapter 3, *The Birthday Card* (page 58), by seeming to mix the cards as you cut them several times.

Leave the pack face down on the table, and put your right hand into your pocket. Scrape the nail of your second finger across the cardboard to get the adhesive under your fingernail.

Bring out the rubber band and hand it to the person, which gives him or her a chance to see that it is unprepared. Ask the person to put the band around the pack of cards, and pick up the pack with your left hand to help hold it upright, so he or she will put the band horizontally around the middle of the pack.

Bring your right hand to the back of the pack to adjust the band, and as you do that, move your fingernail upward against the back of the

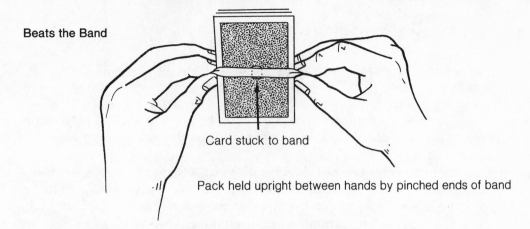

Card stuck to band

Pack held upright between hands by pinched ends of band

rear card (the chosen one) to transfer the adhesive to it. With your right thumb, press the center of the band on the blob of adhesive so the card is firmly stuck to it.

Without stretching the band loose, pinch the right end of it, at the right side of the pack, between your right thumb and first finger. Pinch the other end of the band, at the left side of the pack, in the same way between your left thumb and first finger.

Holding the pack vertically upright between your hands by the two ends of the band, slowly lift it about a foot above the table.

Ask the person to call aloud the name of the card chosen. When that is done, just stretch the band by moving both hands out left and right, and shake it slightly until all the cards fall out, except the chosen one that hangs facing the person inside the stretched-out band.

Keep it held that way a moment. Then relax the band, and take the bottom of the card with your left hand. Bring your right thumb to the back of it, and scrape the adhesive off the card with your thumbnail as you remove the band. Hand the person the card, and put the band away in your pocket.

Test Run

This trick explains how you can use the adhesive to make instantly an impromptu double-faced card with any two cards from a borrowed pack.

Secretly stick a *very small* (pinhead size) pellet of adhesive to the back of the top card of the pack. Place the pack *face up* at the far left side of the table, putting it down gently so it doesn't stick to the tabletop.

Start the trick by spreading the cards out across the table, left to right, in a long face-up row. "Have you a favorite card?" you ask someone. "Just slide any card you choose out of the pack."

When the person has pulled one card out of the spread (for example, the four of hearts), gather up the pack, turn it face down, and hold it in your left hand.

Take the chosen card from the table, *keep it face up*, and place it on top of the face-down pack, which puts it squarely on top of the adhesive on the card beneath it.

Press the chosen card down with your left thumb across the pack, and point to it with your right first finger as you ask the person to make sure he or she remembers it. With the two stuck together back to back, you now have what amounts to a double-faced card.

Draw it back toward you about an inch, take it at the back edge between your right thumb and first finger, and lift it straight upright. Tilt the pack upright, and place the double card at the face of the pack. As you do that, glance at whatever card is stuck to the back of it (for example, the seven of diamonds) and remember it.

Explain that you are going to bury the chosen card so it will be lost in the pack. With your right hand, lift about one-third of the cards off the top, place them face down on the table, then lift off another third, and place those beside the first batch. Place the remainder of the cards, with the chosen card at the face of them, on the second batch. Pick up the first batch, put those on top, square up the pack, and leave it face down on the table.

"I have a favorite card, too," you say. "It's my testing card, the seven of diamonds" (or whatever the card stuck to the back of the chosen card happens to be). "I use it to make sure the magic is working. Let's try a test run."

Snap your fingers, and quickly spread the pack out across the table in a face-down row. The reverse side of the double card appears face up at the center of the spread. "There it is—the seven of diamonds. Flipped itself over. I guess we're all set."

Separate the spread-out pack at the face-up card. Gather all the cards to the right of that card, turn them face up, and hold them squared up in your left hand.

Pick up the double card, keeping it face up, and drop it on top of those in the left hand. Gather up the rest of the cards, square them face up, and drop them on top of the double card. Then turn the whole pack face down and place it back on the table. (Your seven of diamonds is now buried again in the middle of the pack, with the attached chosen card face up.)

"Now that we've had a test run," you say, "let's see if my card can show your card how to flip itself over." Quickly spread out the pack in a face-down row, and show that the chosen card has appeared face up at the center.

"Was that it? The four of hearts?" you ask. "So far, so good. But let's try it the hard way. . . . I'll take your card completely away from the pack and hide it in my pocket."

Slide the double card out of the spread on the table. Pick it up, keep its back toward you, and put it into the right-hand pocket of your jacket. Inside the pocket, separate the two cards by pulling them apart. Feel for the adhesive pellet, scrape it off with a fingernail, and bring your hand out.

Gather up the pack, take it in your left hand, and say, "This time, my card has to flip itself right out of the pack and do some long-distance flying to find yours." Bring your right thumb to the end of the pack, riffle the cards sharply, and then drop the pack on the table. "There it goes!"

Show your right hand is empty, reach into your pocket, take the card that is toward the outside of the pocket, and bring it out to show it. "There's yours, of course. The four of hearts."

Drop that card on the table, and reach into your pocket again. Slowly bring out the other card. "And here's mine . . . my seven of diamonds. It did fly into my pocket to find yours!"

The Magnetic Cup and Straw

If you have a pellet of adhesive hidden behind one of the buttons of your jacket, you will be able to do this trick with any small paper cup and a drinking straw.

Where there are no straws available, you can use one of the little plastic sticks often served for stirring coffee, or a lightweight plastic spoon. Lacking either of those, you can still do the trick with the cup and a pen or pencil taken from your pocket.

You seem to make the straw cling to the opened-out fingertips of first one hand and then the other, as if it were floating there, held by some strange magnetic force.

Then you stand the straw on end in the cup, slowly tilt the cup over, mouth down, and the straw remains suspended in the cup without falling out.

The Magnetic Cup and Straw

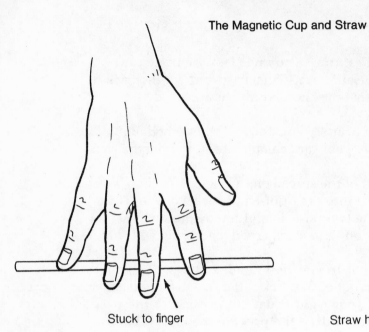

Stuck to finger

Straw clings to fingertips

Straw hangs suspended in upside-down cup

Cup hangs suspended from straw—
swung back and forth

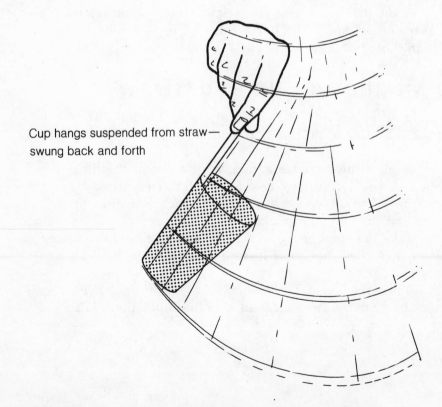

Finally the cup hangs suspended at the bottom end of the straw, and, holding the straw by its top end, you swing the clinging cup back and forth.

Start by secretly getting the adhesive pellet stuck to the tip of your right second finger. Curl that finger and the two below it in toward the palm of your hand, leaving your thumb and first finger free. Place the cup on the table in front of you, and the straw beside it.

Pick up the left end of the straw between your left thumb and first finger. Hold it horizontal. Keep that end held with the left hand, and bring your right thumb and first finger down over the straw to grip it to the right of its center. Press your other right fingertips against the straw so it sticks to the adhesive on the tip of your second finger.

Remove your left hand, and spread open your right fingers and thumb, keeping the hand palm down. The straw seems to cling to your fingertips. Very slowly, move your right hand up and down to show the clinging straw.

Bring your right thumb to the back of the straw to hold it again between thumb and fingers. Hold out your left hand, palm upward. Place the center of the horizontal straw against the tip of your left second finger, and as you do that, roll the straw forward slightly so the adhesive pellet comes free from your right fingertip and sticks to the left fingertip. Press down on the straw to make sure it sticks.

Keep the hands palm to palm and turn both hands over together, with the left-hand palm down on top. Take away the right hand, and slowly spread open the left fingers. The straw now clings to the left fingertips.

Move that hand slowly up and down to show the straw held to the fingertips. Then turn the left palm to the front, with its thumb pointed toward the ceiling, and show the straw clinging vertically to your left fingers. Swing the hand over palm downward again to bring the clinging straw horizontal.

Turn the right-hand palm upward, and bring it up beneath the left palm. With the hands palm to palm, turn them over together, bringing the right hand to the top. As you turn your hands, roll the straw slightly between them to free it from the left fingertip. Take away the straw with your right thumb and fingers.

Pick up the cup with your left hand, turn its mouth toward those watching, to let them see there is nothing inside it, and then hold the cup upright.

With your right hand, put the right end of the straw down inside the cup, also putting your fingers down inside it to stand the straw on end. Press the straw against the side of the cup, secretly sticking the adhesive to it just below the inside of the top rim. (If the cup is shallow, *tilt* the straw instead of standing it upright, so it leans back with the adhesive stuck against the top rim.)

Remove your right hand. Pick up the cup with your left hand. Slowly tilt the cup all the way over to the right until it is mouth down. The straw remains suspended in the cup and doesn't fall out. Shake it a little, and then turn the cup mouth upward again.

Take the top end of the straw between your right thumb and first finger and lift it straight up, so the cup is drawn out of your left hand and hangs suspended at the bottom of the straw. Gently swing it back and forth.

Finally take the bottom of the hanging cup with your left hand, and slide your right thumb and fingers down along the straw to the rim. Roll the straw slightly to detach it from the cup, and remove it, holding the straw with your thumb covering the adhesive pellet.

With your left hand, turn the cup over mouth down, shake it, show it is empty, and drop it to the table. At the same time you are showing the cup, let your right hand swing down to your side momentarily with the straw. Secretly scrape the adhesive off the straw with your fingernail, then bring the straw up and drop that on the table.

INDEX